Connected ❦ Mathematics 2™

Prime Time

Factors and Multiples

Glenda Lappan
James T. Fey
William M. Fitzgerald
Susan N. Friel
Elizabeth Difanis Phillips

PEARSON

Boston, Massachusetts · Glenview, Illinois · Shoreview, Minnesota · Upper Saddle River, New Jersey

Connected Mathematics™ was developed at Michigan State University with financial support from the Michigan State University Office of the Provost, Computing and Technology, and the College of Natural Science.

This material is based upon work supported by the National Science Foundation under Grant No. MDR 9150217 and Grant No. ESI 9986372. Opinions expressed are those of the authors and not necessarily those of the Foundation.

The Michigan State University authors and administration have agreed that all MSU royalties arising from this publication will be devoted to purposes supported by the MSU Mathematics Education Enrichment Fund.

Acknowledgments appear on page 84, which constitutes an extension of this copyright page.

13-digit ISBN 978-0-13-366104-0
10-digit ISBN 0-13-366104-0
1 2 3 4 5 6 7 8 9 10   11 10 09 08

Authors of Connected Mathematics

(from left to right) Glenda Lappan, Betty Phillips, Susan Friel, Bill Fitzgerald, Jim Fey

Glenda Lappan is a University Distinguished Professor in the Department of Mathematics at Michigan State University. Her research and development interests are in the connected areas of students' learning of mathematics and mathematics teachers' professional growth and change related to the development and enactment of K–12 curriculum materials.

James T. Fey is a Professor of Curriculum and Instruction and Mathematics at the University of Maryland. His consistent professional interest has been development and research focused on curriculum materials that engage middle and high school students in problem-based collaborative investigations of mathematical ideas and their applications.

William M. Fitzgerald *(Deceased)* was a Professor in the Department of Mathematics at Michigan State University. His early research was on the use of concrete materials in supporting student learning and led to the development of teaching materials for laboratory environments. Later he helped develop a teaching model to support student experimentation with mathematics.

Susan N. Friel is a Professor of Mathematics Education in the School of Education at the University of North Carolina at Chapel Hill. Her research interests focus on statistics education for middle-grade students and, more broadly, on teachers' professional development and growth in teaching mathematics K–8.

Elizabeth Difanis Phillips is a Senior Academic Specialist in the Mathematics Department of Michigan State University. She is interested in teaching and learning mathematics for both teachers and students. These interests have led to curriculum and professional development projects at the middle school and high school levels, as well as projects related to the teaching and learning of algebra across the grades.

CMP2 Development Staff

Teacher Collaborator in Residence
Yvonne Grant
Michigan State University

Administrative Assistant
Judith Martus Miller
Michigan State University

Production and Field Site Manager
Lisa Keller
Michigan State University

Technical and Editorial Support
Brin Keller, Peter Lappan, Jim Laser,
Michael Masterson, Stacey Miceli

Assessment Team
June Bailey and **Debra Sobko** (Apollo Middle School, Rochester, New York), **George Bright** (University of North Carolina, Greensboro), **Gwen Ranzau Campbell** (Sunrise Park Middle School, White Bear Lake, Minnesota), **Holly DeRosia, Kathy Dole,** and **Teri Keusch** (Portland Middle School, Portland, Michigan), **Mary Beth Schmitt** (Traverse City East Junior High School, Traverse City, Michigan), **Genni Steele** (Central Middle School, White Bear Lake, Minnesota), **Jacqueline Stewart** (Okemos, Michigan), **Elizabeth Tye** (Magnolia Junior High School, Magnolia, Arkansas)

Development Assistants
At Lansing Community College *Undergraduate Assistant:* **James Brinegar**

At Michigan State University *Graduate Assistants:* **Dawn Berk, Emily Bouck, Bulent Buyukbozkirli, Kuo-Liang Chang, Christopher Danielson, Srinivasa Dharmavaram, Deb Johanning, Kelly Rivette, Sarah Sword, Tat Ming Sze, Marie Turini, Jeffrey Wanko;** *Undergraduate Assistants:* **Daniel Briggs, Jeffrey Chapin, Jade Corsé, Elisha Hardy, Alisha Harold, Elizabeth Keusch, Julia Letoutchaia, Karen Loeffler, Brian Oliver, Carl Oliver, Evonne Pedawi, Lauren Rebrovich**

At the University of Maryland *Graduate Assistants:* **Kim Harris Bethea, Kara Karch**

At the University of North Carolina (Chapel Hill) *Graduate Assistants:* **Mark Ellis, Trista Stearns;** *Undergraduate Assistant:* **Daniel Smith**

Advisory Board for CMP2

Thomas Banchoff
Professor of Mathematics
Brown University
Providence, Rhode Island

Anne Bartel
Mathematics Coordinator
Minneapolis Public Schools
Minneapolis, Minnesota

Hyman Bass
Professor of Mathematics
University of Michigan
Ann Arbor, Michigan

Joan Ferrini-Mundy
Associate Dean of the College of Natural Science; Professor
Michigan State University
East Lansing, Michigan

James Hiebert
Professor
University of Delaware
Newark, Delaware

Susan Hudson Hull
Charles A. Dana Center
University of Texas
Austin, Texas

Michele Luke
Mathematics Curriculum
Coordinator
West Junior High
Minnetonka, Minnesota

Kay McClain
Professor of Mathematics
Education
Vanderbilt University
Nashville, Tennessee

Edward Silver
Professor; Chair of Educational
Studies
University of Michigan
Ann Arbor, Michigan

Judith Sowder
Professor Emerita
San Diego State University
San Diego, California

Lisa Usher
Mathematics Resource Teacher
California Academy of
Mathematics and Science
San Pedro, California

Field Test Sites for CMP2

During the development of the revised edition of *Connected Mathematics* (CMP2), more than 100 classroom teachers have field-tested materials at 49 school sites in 12 states and the District of Columbia. This classroom testing occurred over three academic years (2001 through 2004), allowing careful study of the effectiveness of each of the 24 units that comprise the program. A special thanks to the students and teachers at these pilot schools.

Arkansas
Magnolia Public Schools
Kittena Bell*, Judith Trowell*; *Central Elementary School:* Maxine Broom, Betty Eddy, Tiffany Fallin, Bonnie Flurry, Carolyn Monk, Elizabeth Tye; *Magnolia Junior High School:* Monique Bryan, Ginger Cook, David Graham, Shelby Lamkin

Colorado
Boulder Public Schools
Nevin Platt Middle School: Judith Koenig

St. Vrain Valley School District, Longmont
Westview Middle School: Colleen Beyer, Kitty Canupp, Ellie Decker*, Peggy McCarthy, Tanya deNobrega, Cindy Payne, Ericka Pilon, Andrew Roberts

District of Columbia
Capitol Hill Day School: Ann Lawrence

Georgia
University of Georgia, Athens
Brad Findell

Madison Public Schools
Morgan County Middle School: Renee Burgdorf, Lynn Harris, Nancy Kurtz, Carolyn Stewart

Maine
Falmouth Public Schools
Falmouth Middle School: Donna Erikson, Joyce Hebert, Paula Hodgkins, Rick Hogan, David Legere, Cynthia Martin, Barbara Stiles, Shawn Towle*

Michigan
Portland Public Schools
Portland Middle School: Mark Braun, Holly DeRosia, Kathy Dole*, Angie Foote, Teri Keusch, Tammi Wardwell

Traverse City Area Public Schools
Bertha Vos Elementary: Kristin Sak; *Central Grade School:* Michelle Clark; Jody Meyers; *Eastern Elementary:* Karrie Tufts; *Interlochen Elementary:* Mary McGee-Cullen; *Long Lake Elementary:* Julie Faulkner*, Charlie Maxbauer, Katherine Sleder; *Norris Elementary:* Hope Slanaker; *Oak Park Elementary:* Jessica Steed; *Traverse Heights Elementary:* Jennifer Wolfert; *Westwoods Elementary:* Nancy Conn; *Old Mission Peninsula School:* Deb Larimer; *Traverse City East Junior High:* Ivanka Berkshire, Ruthanne Kladder, Jan Palkowski, Jane Peterson, Mary Beth Schmitt; *Traverse City West Junior High:* Dan Fouch*, Ray Fouch

Sturgis Public Schools
Sturgis Middle School: Ellen Eisele

Minnesota
Burnsville School District 191
Hidden Valley Elementary: Stephanie Cin, Jane McDevitt

Hopkins School District 270
Alice Smith Elementary: Sandra Cowing, Kathleen Gustafson, Martha Mason, Scott Stillman; *Eisenhower Elementary:* Chad Bellig, Patrick Berger, Nancy Glades, Kye Johnson, Shane Wasserman, Victoria Wilson; *Gatewood Elementary:* Sarah Ham, Julie Kloos, Janine Pung, Larry Wade; *Glen Lake Elementary:* Jacqueline Cramer, Kathy Hering, Cecelia Morris, Robb Trenda; *Katherine Curren Elementary:* Diane Bancroft, Sue DeWit, John Wilson; *L. H. Tanglen Elementary:* Kevin Athmann, Lisa Becker, Mary LaBelle, Kathy Rezac, Roberta Severson; *Meadowbrook Elementary:* Jan Gauger, Hildy Shank, Jessica Zimmerman; *North Junior High:* Laurel Hahn, Kristin Lee, Jodi Markuson, Bruce Mestemacher, Laurel Miller, Bonnie Rinker, Jeannine Salzer, Sarah Shafer, Cam Stottler; *West Junior High:* Alicia Beebe, Kristie Earl, Nobu Fujii, Pam Georgetti, Susan Gilbert, Regina Nelson Johnson, Debra Lindstrom, Michele Luke*, Jon Sorenson

Minneapolis School District 1
Ann Sullivan K-8 School: Bronwyn Collins; Anne Bartel* (Curriculum and Instruction Office)

Wayzata School District 284
Central Middle School: Sarajane Myers, Dan Nielsen, Tanya Ravnholdt

White Bear Lake School District 624
Central Middle School: Amy Jorgenson, Michelle Reich, Brenda Sammon

New York
New York City Public Schools
IS 89: Yelena Aynbinder, Chi-Man Ng, Nina Rapaport, Joel Spengler, Phyllis Tam*, Brent Wyso; *Wagner Middle School:* Jason Appel, Intissar Fernandez, Yee Gee Get, Richard Goldstein, Irving Marcus, Sue Norton, Bernadita Owens, Jennifer Rehn*, Kevin Yuhas

---

* indicates a Field Test Site Coordinator

Ohio

Talawanda School District, Oxford
Talawanda Middle School: Teresa Abrams, Larry Brock, Heather Brosey, Julie Churchman, Monna Even, Karen Fitch, Bob George, Amanda Klee, Pat Meade, Sandy Montgomery, Barbara Sherman, Lauren Steidl

Miami University
Jeffrey Wanko*

Springfield Public Schools
Rockway School: Jim Mamer

Pennsylvania

Pittsburgh Public Schools
Kenneth Labuskes, Marianne O'Connor, Mary Lynn Raith*; *Arthur J. Rooney Middle School:* David Hairston, Stamatina Mousetis, Alfredo Zangaro; *Frick International Studies Academy:* Suzanne Berry, Janet Falkowski, Constance Finseth, Romika Hodge, Frank Machi; *Reizenstein Middle School:* Jeff Baldwin, James Brautigam, Lorena Burnett, Glen Cobbett, Michael Jordan, Margaret Lazur, Melissa Munnell, Holly Neely, Ingrid Reed, Dennis Reft

Texas

Austin Independent School District
Bedichek Middle School: Lisa Brown, Jennifer Glasscock, Vicki Massey

El Paso Independent School District
Cordova Middle School: Armando Aguirre, Anneliesa Durkes, Sylvia Guzman, Pat Holguin*, William Holguin, Nancy Nava, Laura Orozco, Michelle Peña, Roberta Rosen, Patsy Smith, Jeremy Wolf

Plano Independent School District
Patt Henry, James Wohlgehagen*; *Frankford Middle School:* Mandy Baker, Cheryl Butsch, Amy Dudley, Betsy Eshelman, Janet Greene, Cort Haynes, Kathy Letchworth, Kay Marshall, Kelly McCants, Amy Reck, Judy Scott, Syndy Snyder, Lisa Wang; *Wilson Middle School:* Darcie Bane, Amanda Bedenko, Whitney Evans, Tonelli Hatley, Sarah (Becky) Higgs, Kelly Johnston, Rebecca McElligott, Kay Neuse, Cheri Slocum, Kelli Straight

Washington

Evergreen School District
Shahala Middle School: Nicole Abrahamsen, Terry Coon*, Carey Doyle, Sheryl Drechsler, George Gemma, Gina Helland, Amy Hilario, Darla Lidyard, Sean McCarthy, Tilly Meyer, Willow Neuwelt, Todd Parsons, Brian Pederson, Stan Posey, Shawn Scott, Craig Sjoberg, Lynette Sundstrom, Charles Switzer, Luke Youngblood

Wisconsin

Beaver Dam Unified School District
Beaver Dam Middle School: Jim Braemer, Jeanne Frick, Jessica Greatens, Barbara Link, Dennis McCormick, Karen Michels, Nancy Nichols*, Nancy Palm, Shelly Stelsel, Susan Wiggins

Milwaukee Public Schools
Fritsche Middle School: Peggy Brokaw, Rosann Hollinger*, Dan Homontowski, David Larson, LaRon Ramsey, Judy Roschke*, Lora Ruedt, Dorothy Schuller, Sandra Wiesen, Aaron Womack, Jr.

---

* indicates a Field Test Site Coordinator

Reviews of CMP to Guide Development of CMP2

Before writing for CMP2 began or field tests were conducted, the first edition of *Connected Mathematics* was submitted to the mathematics faculties of school districts from many parts of the country and to 80 individual reviewers for extensive comments.

School District Survey Reviews of CMP

Arizona
Madison School District #38 (Phoenix)

Arkansas
Cabot School District, Little Rock School District, Magnolia School District

California
Los Angeles Unified School District

Colorado
St. Vrain Valley School District (Longmont)

Florida
Leon County Schools (Tallahassee)

Illinois
School District #21 (Wheeling)

Indiana
Joseph L. Block Junior High (East Chicago)

Kentucky
Fayette County Public Schools (Lexington)

Maine
Selection of Schools

Massachusetts
Selection of Schools

Michigan
Sparta Area Schools

Minnesota
Hopkins School District

Texas
Austin Independent School District, The El Paso Collaborative for Academic Excellence, Plano Independent School District

Wisconsin
Platteville Middle School

Individual Reviewers of CMP

Arkansas
Deborah Cramer; Robby Frizzell *(Taylor)*; Lowell Lynde *(University of Arkansas, Monticello)*; Leigh Manzer *(Norfork)*; Lynne Roberts *(Emerson High School, Emerson)*; Tony Timms *(Cabot Public Schools)*; Judith Trowell *(Arkansas Department of Higher Education)*

California
José Alcantar *(Gilroy)*; Eugenie Belcher *(Gilroy)*; Marian Pasternack *(Lowman M. S. T. Center, North Hollywood)*; Susana Pezoa *(San Jose)*; Todd Rabusin *(Hollister)*; Margaret Siegfried *(Ocala Middle School, San Jose)*; Polly Underwood *(Ocala Middle School, San Jose)*

Colorado
Janeane Golliher *(St. Vrain Valley School District, Longmont)*; Judith Koenig *(Nevin Platt Middle School, Boulder)*

Florida
Paige Loggins *(Swift Creek Middle School, Tallahassee)*

Illinois
Jan Robinson *(School District #21, Wheeling)*

Indiana
Frances Jackson *(Joseph L. Block Junior High, East Chicago)*

Kentucky
Natalee Feese *(Fayette County Public Schools, Lexington)*

Maine
Betsy Berry *(Maine Math & Science Alliance, Augusta)*

Maryland
Joseph Gagnon *(University of Maryland, College Park)*; Paula Maccini *(University of Maryland, College Park)*

Massachusetts
George Cobb *(Mt. Holyoke College, South Hadley)*; Cliff Kanold *(University of Massachusetts, Amherst)*

Michigan
Mary Bouck *(Farwell Area Schools)*; Carol Dorer *(Slauson Middle School, Ann Arbor)*; Carrie Heaney *(Forsythe Middle School, Ann Arbor)*; Ellen Hopkins *(Clague Middle School, Ann Arbor)*; Teri Keusch *(Portland Middle School, Portland)*; Valerie Mills *(Oakland Schools, Waterford)*; Mary Beth Schmitt *(Traverse City East Junior High, Traverse City)*; Jack Smith *(Michigan State University, East Lansing)*; Rebecca Spencer *(Sparta Middle School, Sparta)*; Ann Marie Nicoll Turner *(Tappan Middle School, Ann Arbor)*; Scott Turner *(Scarlett Middle School, Ann Arbor)*

Minnesota
Margarita Alvarez *(Olson Middle School, Minneapolis)*; Jane Amundson *(Nicollet Junior High, Burnsville)*; Anne Bartel *(Minneapolis Public Schools)*; Gwen Ranzau Campbell *(Sunrise Park Middle School, White Bear Lake)*; Stephanie Cin *(Hidden Valley Elementary, Burnsville)*; Joan Garfield *(University of Minnesota, Minneapolis)*; Gretchen Hall *(Richfield Middle School, Richfield)*; Jennifer Larson *(Olson Middle School, Minneapolis)*; Michele Luke *(West Junior High, Minnetonka)*; Jeni Meyer *(Richfield Junior High, Richfield)*; Judy Pfingsten *(Inver Grove Heights Middle School, Inver Grove Heights)*; Sarah Shafer *(North Junior High, Minnetonka)*; Genni Steele *(Central Middle School, White Bear Lake)*; Victoria Wilson *(Eisenhower Elementary, Hopkins)*; Paul Zorn *(St. Olaf College, Northfield)*

New York
Debra Altenau-Bartolino *(Greenwich Village Middle School, New York)*; Doug Clements *(University of Buffalo)*; Francis Curcio *(New York University, New York)*; Christine Dorosh *(Clinton School for Writers, Brooklyn)*; Jennifer Rehn *(East Side Middle School, New York)*; Phyllis Tam *(IS 89 Lab School, New York)*;

Marie Turini *(Louis Armstrong Middle School, New York)*; Lucy West *(Community School District 2, New York)*; Monica Witt *(Simon Baruch Intermediate School 104, New York)*

Pennsylvania
Robert Aglietti *(Pittsburgh)*; Sharon Mihalich *(Pittsburgh)*; Jennifer Plumb *(South Hills Middle School, Pittsburgh)*; Mary Lynn Raith *(Pittsburgh Public Schools)*

Texas
Michelle Bittick *(Austin Independent School District)*; Margaret Cregg *(Plano Independent School District)*; Sheila Cunningham *(Klein Independent School District)*; Judy Hill *(Austin Independent School District)*; Patricia Holguin *(El Paso Independent School District)*; Bonnie McNemar *(Arlington)*; Kay Neuse *(Plano Independent School District)*; Joyce Polanco *(Austin Independent School District)*; Marge Ramirez *(University of Texas at El Paso)*; Pat Rossman *(Baker Campus, Austin)*; Cindy Schimek *(Houston)*; Cynthia Schneider *(Charles A. Dana Center, University of Texas at Austin)*; Uri Treisman *(Charles A. Dana Center, University of Texas at Austin)*; Jacqueline Weilmuenster *(Grapevine-Colleyville Independent School District)*; LuAnn Weynand *(San Antonio)*; Carmen Whitman *(Austin Independent School District)*; James Wohlgehagen *(Plano Independent School District)*

Washington
Ramesh Gangolli *(University of Washington, Seattle)*

Wisconsin
Susan Lamon *(Marquette University, Hales Corner)*; Steve Reinhart *(retired, Chippewa Falls Middle School, Eau Claire)*

Table of Contents

Prime Time
Factors and Multiples

Prime Time

Factors and Multiples

Why is it convenient to measure time using 60 minutes in an hour (not 59 or 61) and 24 hours in a day (not 23 or 25)?

Insects called cicadas (si KAY dahs) spend most of their lives underground. Many come above ground only every 13 years or 17 years. Why is it unlikely you will ever see 13-year and 17-year cicadas appear together?

Why does your birthday fall on a different day of the week from one year to the next? Why is the same also true for New Year's Day and the Fourth of July?

Think for a minute about some of the ways in which you use numbers. You use numbers to count, to measure, to make comparisons, and to describe where places are located. Numbers help you communicate, find information, use technology, and make purchases. Numbers can also help you think about situations such as those on the previous page.

Whole numbers have interesting properties and structures you may not have thought about. For example, some numbers can be divided evenly by many numbers, while others can be divided evenly by only a few numbers. Some pairs of numbers have lots of factors in common, while others share only one factor. The investigations in *Prime Time* will help you learn to use ideas about the structure of numbers to explain some curious patterns, to solve problems, and to think about some interesting questions, such as those on the previous page.

Mathematical Highlights

Factors and Multiples

In *Prime Time,* you will explore important properties of whole numbers, especially properties related to multiplication and division.

You will learn how to

- Understand relationships among factors, multiples, divisors, and products

- Recognize and use properties of prime and composite numbers, even and odd numbers, and square numbers

- Use rectangles to represent the factor pairs of numbers

- Develop strategies for finding factors and multiples, least common multiples, and greatest common factors

- Recognize and use the fact that every whole number can be written in exactly one way as a product of prime numbers

- Use factors and multiples to solve problems and to explain some numerical facts of everyday life

- Develop a variety of strategies for solving problems—building models, making lists and tables, drawing diagrams, and solving simpler problems

When you encounter a new math problem, ask yourself questions about the numbers and relationships involved in the problem. In this unit, you might ask questions such as these:

Will breaking a number into factors help me solve the problem?

What relationships will doing that help me see?

What do the factors and multiples of the numbers tell me about the situation?

How can I find the factors of the numbers?

How can I find the multiples?

What common factors and common multiples do the numbers have?

Unit Project

My Special Number

Many people have a number that they think is interesting. Choose a whole number between 10 and 100 that you especially like.

In your notebook:

• record your number

• explain why you chose that number

• list three or four mathematical facts about your number

• list three or four connections you can make between your number and your world

As you work through the investigations in *Prime Time*, you will learn a lot about numbers. Think about how these new ideas apply to your special number. Add any new information about your number to your notebook. You may want to designate one or two "special-number" pages in your notebook, to record this information. At the end of the unit, your teacher will ask you to find an interesting way to report to the class about your special number.

Factors and Products

Jamie is 12 years old. Her cousin, Emilio, is 2 years old. Her brother, Cam, is 3. Her neighbor, Esther, is 8. The following number sentences say that Jamie is

6 times as old as Emilio,   4 times as old as Cam,   and $1\frac{1}{2}$ times as old as Esther.

$$12 = 6 \times 2$$ $$12 = 4 \times 3$$ $$12 = 1\frac{1}{2} \times 8$$

Notice that each of the whole numbers 2, 3, 4, and 6 can be multiplied by another whole number to get 12. For this reason, 2, 3, 4, and 6 are called *whole-number factors*, or *whole-number divisors*, of 12.

Although 8 *is* a whole number, it *is not* a whole-number factor of 12 because you cannot multiply 8 by another whole number to get 12.

To save time, we will simply use the words **factor** and **divisor** to refer to whole-number factors and whole-number divisors of a number.

Playing the Factor Game

Playing the Factor Game is a fun way to practice finding factors of whole numbers. If you pay close attention, you may learn some interesting things about numbers that you didn't know before! To play the game, you need a Factor Game Board and colored pens, pencils, or markers.

active math
online

For: Factor Game Activity
Visit: PHSchool.com
Web Code: amd-1101

The Factor Game

1	2	3	4	5
6	7	8	9	10
11	12	13	14	15
16	17	18	19	20
21	22	23	24	25
26	27	28	29	30

Factor Game Rules

1. Player A chooses a number on the game board and circles it.

2. Using a different color, Player B circles all the proper factors of Player A's number. The **proper factors** of a number are all the factors of that number, except the number itself. For example, the proper factors of 12 are 1, 2, 3, 4, and 6. Although 12 is a factor of itself, it is not a proper factor.

3. Player B circles a new number, and Player A circles all the factors of the number that are not already circled.

4. The players take turns choosing numbers and circling factors.

5. If a player circles a number that has no factors left that have not been circled, then that player does not get the points for the number circled and loses the next turn.

6. The game ends when there are no numbers left with uncircled factors.

7. Each player adds the numbers that are circled with his or her color. The player with the greater total is the winner.

The First Five Moves of a Sample Game

This table shows the first five moves of a game between Cathy and Keiko.
The first column describes the moves the players made. The other columns
show the game board and the score after each move.

Action	Game Board	Score
Cathy circles 24. Keiko circles 1, 2, 3, 4, 6, 8, and 12 (the proper factors of 24).	Board with 1, 2, 3, 4 (circled), 6, 8, 12, 24 circled	Cathy 24 / Keiko 36
Keiko circles 28. Cathy circles 7 and 14 (the factors of 28 that are not already circled).	Board with 1, 2, 3, 4, 6, 7, 8, 12, 14, 24, 28 circled	Cathy 24, 21 / Keiko 36, 28
Cathy circles 27. Keiko circles 9 (the only factor of 27 that is not already circled).	Board with 1, 2, 3, 4, 6, 7, 8, 9, 12, 14, 24, 27, 28 circled	Cathy 24, 21, 27 / Keiko 36, 28, 9
Keiko circles 30. Cathy circles 5,10 and 15 (the factors of 30 that are not already circled).	Board with 1, 2, 3, 4, 5, 6, 7, 8, 9, 10, 12, 14, 15, 24, 27, 28, 30 circled	Cathy 24, 21, 27, 30 / Keiko 36, 28, 9, 30
Cathy circles 25. All the factors of 25 are circled. Cathy does not receive any points for this turn and loses her next turn.	Board with 1, 2, 3, 4, 5, 6, 7, 8, 9, 10, 12, 14, 15, 24, 25, 27, 28, 30 circled	Cathy 24, 21, 27, 30, 0 / Keiko 36, 28, 9, 30, 0

Problem 1.1 Finding Proper Factors

A. Play the Factor Game several times with a partner. Take turns making the first move. Look for moves that will give you more points than your opponent. As you play, write down any strategies or patterns you find.

B. How can you test to determine whether a number is a factor of another number?

C. If you know a factor of a number, can you find another factor? Explain your thinking.

D. Give an example of a number that has many factors and an example of a number that has few factors.

E. Make a list of the factors of 18. Make a list of the divisors of 18. Are the factors of a number also divisors of the number? Explain your thinking.

F. How do you know when you have found all the factors of a number?

ACE Homework starts on page 14.

1.2 Playing to Win the Factor Game

Did you notice that some numbers are better than others to choose for the first move in the Factor Game? For example, if you choose 22, you get 22 points and your opponent gets only $1 + 2 + 11 = 14$ points. However, if you choose 18, you get 18 points, and your opponent gets $1 + 2 + 3 + 6 + 9 = 21$ points!

Now you will make a table to analyze the Factor Game and look for patterns. Your table might start like this:

First Move	Proper Factors	My Score	Opponent's Score
1	None	Lose a Turn	0
2	1	2	1
3	1	3	1
4	1, 2	4	3

Problem 1.2 Prime and Composite Numbers

A. 1. Make a table of all the possible first moves (numbers from 1 to 30) in the Factor Game.

2. For each move, list the proper factors of the number, and record the scores you and your opponent would receive.

3. Describe an interesting pattern you see in your table.

B. What is the best first move? Why?

C. Which first move would make you lose your next turn? Why?

D. Other than your answer to Question C, what is the worst first move? Why?

E. List all the first moves that allow your opponent to score only one point. These numbers are called *prime numbers*.

F. Are all prime numbers good first moves? Explain. (Remember, a number is a *good first move* if the player choosing the number scores more points than his or her opponent.)

G. List all the first moves that allow your opponent to score more than one point. These numbers also have a special name. They are called *composite numbers*.

H. Are composite numbers good first moves? Explain.

ACE Homework starts on page 14.

Did You Know?

Large prime numbers are used to encode top-secret information. In 1999, Nayan Hajratwala found a prime number with more than 2 million digits. In type this size, that number would be more than 2 miles long! The Electronic Frontier Foundation awarded Mr. Hajratwala $50,000 for discovering the first prime number with more than 1,000,000 digits. The EFF now offers a prize of $250,000 to the first person to find a prime number with over 1,000,000,000 digits!

Mathematicians have always been puzzled about fast ways of determining whether really big numbers are prime. In August, 2002, Dr. Manindra Agrawal and two college students, Neeraj Kayal and Nitin Saxena, made a breakthrough. They surprised and delighted mathematicians with an elegant way of determining whether really huge numbers are prime. You can find more information about this in the August 8, 2002, issue of *The New York Times*.

Go Online
PHSchool.com   **For:** Information about prime numbers
Web Code: ame-9031

1.3 The Product Game

You learned about factors of a number in Problems 1.1 and 1.2. In the next game you will learn about multiples of numbers. A **multiple** of a number is the product of that number and another whole number. For example, 24 is a multiple of 6 because $4 \times 6 = 24$. Multiples and factors have an interesting back-and-forth relationship.

If a number is a multiple of 5, then 5 is a factor of that number. These five sentences describe how the numbers 3, 5, and 15 are related.

$$5 \times 3 = 15$$

5 is a factor of 15.

3 is a factor of 15.

15 is a multiple of 5.

15 is a multiple of 3.

You can probably think of other ways to show the relationship. For example, you could add these to the list:

15 is divisible by 5.

15 is divisible by 3.

In the Factor Game, you start with a number and find its factors. In the Product Game, you start with factors and find their product. The Product Game board consists of a list of factors and a grid of products. The object is to mark four products in a row—up and down, across, or diagonally—before your opponent does.

active math
online

For: Product Game Activity
Visit: PHSchool.com
Web Code: amd-1103

The Product Game

1	2	3	4	5	6
7	8	9	10	12	14
15	16	18	20	21	24
25	27	28	30	32	35
36	40	42	45	48	49
54	56	63	64	72	81

Factors:

1 2 3 4 5 6 7 8 9

To play the game, you need a Product Game Board, two paper clips, and colored markers or chips—one color for each player.

Product Game Rules

1. Player A puts a paper clip on a number in the factor list. Player A does not mark a square on the product grid because only one factor has been marked. It takes two factors to make a product.

2. Player B puts the other paper clip on any number in the factor list (including the same number marked by Player A). Player B then shades or covers the product of the two factors on the product grid. An example is shown on the next page.

3. Player A moves *either* paper clip to another number, leaving one in its original place, and then shades or covers the new product.

4. Each player, in turn, moves a paper clip and marks a product. If a product is already marked, the player does not get a mark for that turn. The winner is the first player to mark four squares in a row—up and down, across, or diagonally.

Problem 1.3 Finding Multiples

A. Play the Product Game several times with a partner. Look for interesting patterns and strategies that might help you win. Make notes on your observations.

B. Examine the Product Game Board. Is it possible to get every number on the product grid by multiplying two of the numbers in the factor list? Justify your answer.

C. Can you find two numbers in the list of factors for the game whose product is *not* on the product grid?

D. Suppose that a game is in progress and you want to cover the number 12 on the grid. Describe one way this can happen. Can you get 12 in more than one way?

E. 1. Suppose that a game is in progress and one of the paper clips is on 5. What products can you make by moving the other paper clip?

   2. List five multiples of 5 that are not on the game board.

 Homework starts on page 14.

The Product Game

1	2	3	4	5	6
7	8	9	10	12	14
15	16	18	20	21	24
25	27	28	30	32	35
36	40	42	45	48	49
54	56	63	64	72	81

Factors:

1 2 3 4 5 6 7 8 9

How can I get 12?

Applications

1. Ben claims that 12 is a factor of 24. How can you check to determine whether he is correct?

2. What factor is paired with 6 to give 24?

3. What factor is paired with 5 to give 45?

4. What factor is paired with 3 to give 24?

5. What factor is paired with 6 to give 54?

6. How would you test to see whether 7 is a factor of 291?

7. **Multiple Choice** Which of these numbers has the most factors?

   A. 6   **B.** 17   **C.** 25   **D.** 36

8. Lareina understands factors, but sometimes she has trouble finding all the factors of a number. What advice would you give to help her find all the factors of a number? Demonstrate by finding all the factors of 110.

9. Find two numbers that have 2, 3, and 5 as factors. What other factors do the two numbers have in common?

10. **a.** What do you get when you use your calculator to divide 84 by 14? What does this tell you about 14 and 84?

    b. What do you get when you use your calculator to divide 84 by 15? What does this tell you about 15 and 84?

11. Ramona says the Factor Game might also be called the Divisor Game. Do you agree? Why or why not?

12. a. Is 6 a divisor of 18? Why or why not?

b. Is 18 a divisor of 6? Why or why not?

13. Which of these numbers are divisors of 64?

2   6   8   12   16

14. In Exercise 13, Evan noticed that some of the proper factors of 64 can be multiplied to get another proper factor of 64. For example, 2 and 8 are factors of 64, and 16 is also a factor of 64. Does every number have some factors for which this is true?

For: Help with Exercise 14
Web Code: ame-1114

15. a. A prime number has exactly two factors, 1 and itself. If you circle a prime number in the Factor Game, your opponent will receive at most one point. Explain why. Give some examples.

b. A composite number has more than two factors. If you circle a composite number in the Factor Game, your opponent might receive more points than you. Explain why. Give some examples.

16. Why is the set of factors of a number not the same as the set of proper factors of that number?

17. Using the terms *factor*, *divisor*, *multiple*, *product*, and *divisible by*, write as many statements as you can about the number sentence $4 \times 7 = 28$.

18. Dewayne and Todd are playing the Product Game. Dewayne's markers are on 16, 18, and 28, and Todd's markers are on 14, 21, and 30. The paper clips are on 5 and 6. It is Dewayne's turn to move a paper clip.

a. List the moves Dewayne can make.

b. Which move(s) would give Dewayne three markers in a row?

c. Which move(s) would allow him to block Todd?

d. Which move do you think Dewayne should make? Explain.

The Product Game

1	2	3	4	5	6
7	8	9	10	12	14
15	16	18	20	21	24
25	27	28	30	32	35
36	40	42	45	48	49
54	56	63	64	72	81

Factors:

1   2   3   4   5   6   7   8   9

19. a. Suppose that one paper clip on the Product Game board is on 3. What products can you make by moving the other paper clip?

   b. List five multiples of 3 that are not on the game board.

   c. How many multiples of 3 are there?

20. Davis just marked 18 on the Product Game board. On which factors might the paper clips be placed? List all the possibilities.

21. Find two products on the Product Game board, other than 18, that can be made in more than one way. List all the pairs of factors that give each product.

22. Multiple Choice Which set represents all the factors of 12?

   F. {1, 2, 3, 4, 6, 12}   **G.** {12, 24, 36, 48, . . . }
   H. {0, 1, 2, 3, 4, 6, 12}   **J.** {1, 2, 3, 4, 6}

23. Use the ideas from this investigation to list at least five facts about the number 30.

24. Determine whether each of the following numbers can be made in more than one way in the Product Game. State whether the number is prime or composite.

   a. 36   **b.** 5   **c.** 7   **d.** 9

25. Salvador said that the Product Game might also be called the Multiple Game. Do you agree? Why or why not?

26. On the Product Game board, which number is both a prime number and an even number?

27. Jose says the Factor Game and the Product Game are similar because both involve multiplication. Marcus says they are not similar. With whom do you agree and why?

Connections

28. Twenty-five classes from Martin Luther King Elementary School will play the Factor Game at their math carnival. Each class has 32 students. How many game boards are needed if each pair of students is to play the game once?

29. As part of the carnival, the school will hold a Factor Game marathon. It takes Archie and Kel an average of 12 minutes to finish one game. About how many games will they finish if they play nonstop from 9:00 A.M. to 2:30 P.M.?

30. Multiple Choice This week Carlos read a book for language arts class. He finished the book on Friday. On Monday he read 27 pages; on Tuesday he read 31 pages; and on Wednesday he read 28 pages. On Thursday and Friday he read the same number of pages each day. The book had 144 pages. How many pages did he read on Thursday?

A. 28   **B.** 29   **C.** 31   **D.** 58

31. Write a problem like Exercise 30 about a book you have read recently.

32. Long ago, people observed the sun's rising and setting over and over at about equal intervals. They decided to use the amount of time between two sunrises as the length of a day. They divided the day into 24 hours. Use what you know about factors to answer these questions:

a. Why is 24 a more convenient choice for the number of hours in a day than 23 or 25?

b. If you could select a number different from 24 to represent the number of hours in a day, what number would you choose? Why?

33. a. In developing the ways in which we calculate time, astronomers divided an hour into 60 minutes. Why is 60 a good choice (better than 59 or 61)?

   b. If you could select another number to represent the number of minutes in an hour, what would be a good choice? Why?

34. a. Is 132 divisible by 12? By 3? By 4?

   b. Is 160 divisible by 10? By 2? By 5?

   c. Is 42 divisible by 6? By 3? By 2?

   d. What patterns do you see in parts (a), (b), and (c)?

Go Online
PHSchool.com

For: Multiple-Choice Skills Practice
Web Code: ama-1154

For Exercises 35–37, find two numbers that can be multiplied to give each product. Do not use 1 as one of the numbers.

35. 84   **36.** 145   **37.** 300

38. a. Ms. Diaz wants to divide her class of 30 students into 10 groups, not necessarily of equal size. What are some of her choices?

   b. Ms. Diaz wants to divide her class of 30 students into equal-sized groups. What are her choices?

   c. How is the thinking you did in part (a) different from the thinking you did in part (b)?

Extensions

39. Jocelyn and Moesha decide to play the Factor Game on a 100-board, which includes the whole numbers from 1 to 100.

   a. What will Jocelyn's score be if Moesha chooses 100 as her first move?

   b. What will Jocelyn's score be if Moesha chooses 99 as her first move?

   c. What is the best first move on a 100-board?

40. What is my number?

   Clue 1 When you divide my number by 5, the remainder is 4.

   Clue 2 My number has two digits, and both digits are even.

   Clue 3 The sum of the digits is 10.

41. The Factor Game can be played on a 49-board, which includes the whole numbers from 1 to 49.

    a. Use your table for analyzing first moves on a 30-board from Problem 1.2. Extend it to include all the numbers on a 49-board.

    b. What new primes do you find?

The Factor Game

1	2	3	4	5	6	7
8	9	10	11	12	13	14
15	16	17	18	19	20	21
22	23	24	25	26	27	28
29	30	31	32	33	34	35
36	37	38	39	40	41	42
43	44	45	46	47	48	49

42. Lana and Luis are playing the Factor Game on a 49-board. Lana has the first move and chooses 49.

    a. How many points does Luis score for this round?

    b. How many points does Lana score for this round?

43. What is the best first move on a 49-board? Why?

44. What is the worst first move on a 49-board? Why?

45. What three factors were used to make this Product Game board? What product is missing from the grid?

4	6	9
14	?	49

Factors:
___ ___ ___

46. What four factors were used to make this Product Game board? What product is missing from the grid?

9	15	18	
21	?	30	35
	36	42	49

Factors:
___ ___ ___ ___

47. The sum of the proper factors of a number may be greater than, less than, or equal to the number. Ancient mathematicians used this idea to classify numbers as *abundant*, *deficient*, and *perfect*. Each whole number greater than 1 falls into one of these three categories.

a. Draw and label three circles as shown below. The numbers 12, 15, and 6 have been placed in the appropriate circles. Use your factor table to determine what each label means. Then, write each whole number from 2 to 30 in the correct circle.

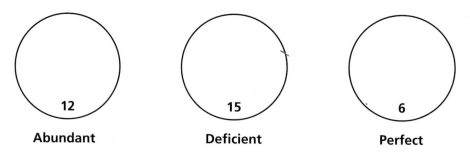

12	15	6
Abundant	**Deficient**	**Perfect**

b. Do the labels seem appropriate? Why or why not?

c. In which circle would 36 belong?

d. In which circle would 55 belong?

48. Look at the Product Game board you used in Problem 1.3. Which of the numbers on that board can be formed by placing both paper clips on the same number? These numbers are called *square numbers*. Why do you think they have this name?

49. a. Suppose you choose 16 as a first move in the Factor Game. How many points does your opponent get? How does your opponent's score for this turn compare to yours?

b. Suppose you choose 4 as a first move. How many points does your opponent get? How does your opponent's score for this turn compare to yours?

c. Find some other numbers that have the same pattern of scoring as 4 and 16. These numbers could be called *near-perfect numbers*. Why do you think this name fits?

Is there a largest perfect number? Mathematicians have been trying for hundreds of years to find the answer to this question. You might like to know that the next largest perfect number after 6 and 28 is 496.

For: Information about perfect numbers
Web Code: ame-9031

Mathematical Reflections 1

In this investigation, you played and analyzed the Factor Game and the Product Game. These questions will help you summarize what you have learned.

Think about your answers to these questions. Discuss your ideas with other students and your teacher. Then write a summary of your findings in your notebook.

1. What are the factors of a number and how do you find them?

2. What did you learn about prime numbers and composite numbers while you were playing the Factor Game? Is the number 1 prime or composite? Explain.

3. What are the multiples of a number and how do you find them?

Unit Project   What's Next?

Write something new that you have learned about your special number now that you have played the Factor Game and the Product Game.

Would your special number be a good first move in either game? Why or why not?

Investigation 2

Whole-Number Patterns and Relationships

Because you have been using whole numbers since you were young, you may think there is not much more to learn about them. However, there are many interesting relationships involving whole numbers that you may never have considered. To notice these relationships, it is sometimes helpful to break whole numbers into factors or to multiply them by other numbers.

Finding Patterns

In the Factor Game and the Product Game, you found that factors occur in pairs. Once you know one factor of a number, you can find another factor. For example, 3 is a factor of 12, and because $3 \times 4 = 12$, 4 is also a factor of 12. We call the pair 3, 4 a **factor pair.**

Every year, Meridian Shopping Mall has an exhibit of arts and crafts. People who want to display their work rent a space for $20 per square yard. Exhibitors are given carpet squares to lay out their spaces. Each carpet square measures 1 square yard. All exhibit spaces must have a rectangular shape.

Terrapin Crafts wants to rent a space of 12 square yards. Use 12 square tiles to represent the carpet squares.

- What are all the possible ways the Terrapin Crafts owner can arrange the squares to make a rectangle?

- How are the rectangles you found and the factors of 12 related?

You just found all the possible rectangles that can be made from 12 tiles. These rectangles are *models* for the number 12. The models are useful because they allow you to "see" the factors of 12. You can make rectangle models such as these for any whole number.

In Problem 2.1, you and your classmates will use grid paper to create all the possible rectangle models for all the whole numbers from 1 to 30. When the rectangles are displayed, you can look for interesting patterns.

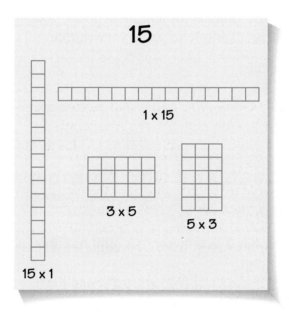

Your teacher will assign your group a few of the numbers from 1 to 30. Work with your group to decide how to distribute the numbers you have been assigned.

Problem 2.1 Rectangles and Factor Pairs

A. From grid paper, cut out all the possible rectangle models you can make for each of your numbers. You may want to use tiles to help you find the rectangles.

Write each number at the top of a sheet of paper, and tape all the rectangles for that number to the sheet. List the factors of the number from least to greatest at the bottom of the paper.

Display the sheets of rectangles in order from 1 to 30 around the room. When all the numbers are displayed, look for patterns.

B. 1. Which numbers have the most rectangles? What kind of numbers are these?

2. Which numbers have the fewest rectangles? What kind of numbers are these?

3. Which numbers are **square numbers** (numbers whose tiles can be arranged to form a square)?

4. How can you use the rectangle models for a number to list the factors of the number? Use an example to show your thinking.

ACE Homework starts on page 30.

2.2 Reasoning With Even and Odd Numbers

An **even number** is a number that has 2 as a factor. An **odd number** is a number that does not have 2 as a factor.

Tilo makes models for whole numbers by arranging square tiles in a special pattern. Here are Lilo's tile models for the numbers from 1 to 7.

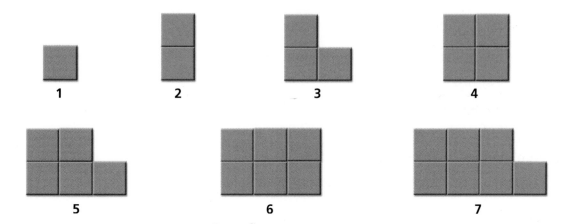

- How are the models of even numbers different from the models of odd numbers?
- Describe the models for 50 and 99.

When you tell what you think will happen in a mathematical situation, you are making a conjecture. A **conjecture** is your best guess about a pattern or a relationship that you observe. You can use models, drawings, or other kinds of evidence to support your conjectures.

Make a conjecture about what happens when you add two even numbers. Do you get an even number or an odd number? Why?

Problem 2.2 asks you to think of other conjectures to make about even and odd numbers.

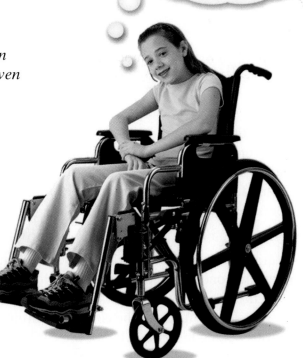

When I add two even numbers, the sum is...

Problem 2.2 Reasoning with Even and Odd Numbers

A. Make conjectures about whether the results below will be even or odd. Then use tile models or some other method to support your conjectures.

   1. the sum of two even numbers

   2. the sum of two odd numbers

   3. the sum of an even number and an odd number

   4. the product of two even numbers

   5. the product of two odd numbers

   6. the product of an even number and an odd number

B. Is 0 an even number or an odd number? How do you know?

C. Without building a tile model, how can you determine whether a sum of numbers, such as $127 + 38$, is even or odd?

D. A problem occurs when we compute $6 + 3 \times 9$. You can get 81 or 33 as the answer! How can you get 81? How can you get 33? The *order of operations* rule says that you do all multiplications and divisions before you add or subtract. This makes 33 the correct answer.

Compute each number and tell whether it is even or odd.

   1. $3 + 5 \times 7$ **2.** $25 - 3 \times 2$ **3.** $11 \times 5 + 3 \times 9$

   4. $43 - 25 \div 5 + 2$ **5.** $43 - 7 + 5 \times 2$ **6.** $6 + 18 - 24 \div 6$

ACE Homework starts on page 30.

2.3 Classifying Numbers

A **Venn diagram** uses circles to group things that belong together. You can use Venn diagrams to explore relationships among whole numbers. For example, suppose that you want to group the whole numbers from 1 to 9 according to whether they are prime or multiples of 2. First, list the numbers that fall into each category:

   Prime Numbers: 2, 3, 5, 7   Multiples of 2: 2, 4, 6, 8

Next, draw and label two overlapping circles, one that represents the prime numbers and one that represents the multiples of 2. Put each number from 1 to 9 in the appropriate region. The numbers that don't fall into either category belong outside of the circles. The numbers that are in both categories belong in the overlap of the circles.

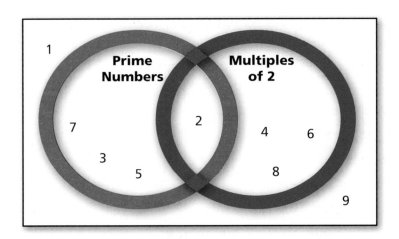

Problem 2.3 **Classifying Numbers**

The Venn diagrams in Questions A–D are related to the ideas you studied in Investigation 1.

A. List the factors of 30 and 36. Fill in a copy of this Venn diagram with all whole numbers less than or equal to 40. Then answer the questions below.

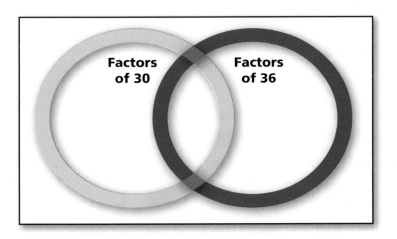

1. What do the numbers in the intersection (the "overlap") of the circular regions have in common?

2. List five numbers that fall in the region outside the circles and explain why they belong outside the circles.

3. Explain how you can use your completed diagram to find the greatest factor that 30 and 36 have in common. What is this *greatest common factor*?

4. What is the least number that falls in the intersection?

B. List the factors of 20 and the factors of 27. Fill in a copy of this Venn diagram with whole numbers less than or equal to 30. Then answer the questions below.

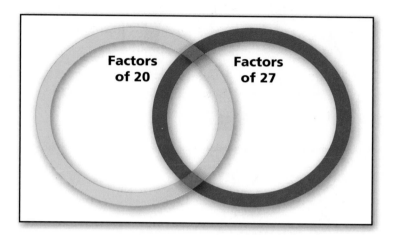

1. What do the numbers in the intersection of the circular regions have in common?

2. Explain how you can use your completed diagram to find the greatest factor that 20 and 27 have in common. What is this greatest common factor?

3. Compare this Venn diagram to the one you completed in Question A. How are they alike, and how are they different?

C. List the multiples of 5 and the multiples of 4 that are less than or equal to 40. Fill in a copy of this Venn diagram with whole numbers less than or equal to 40. Then answer the questions that follow.

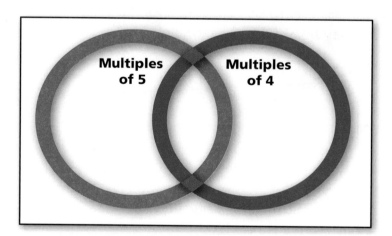

1. What do the numbers in the intersection of the circular regions have in common?

2. Explain how you can use your completed diagram to find the least multiple that 5 and 4 have in common. What is this *least common multiple*?

3. List five more numbers that would be in the intersection if numbers greater than 40 were allowed. What would be the greatest possible number in the intersection if you could use any number?

D. List the multiples of 6 and the multiples of 8 that are less than or equal to 48. Fill in a copy of this Venn diagram with whole numbers less than or equal to 48. Then answer the questions below.

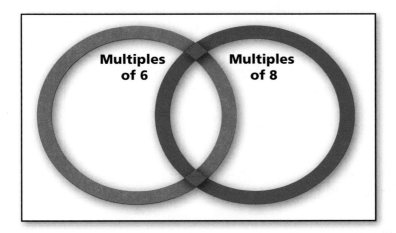

1. What do the numbers in the intersection have in common?

2. Explain how you can use your completed diagram to find the least multiple that 6 and 8 have in common. What is this least common multiple?

3. Compare this Venn diagram to the one you completed in Question C. How are they alike? How are they different?

ACE **Homework starts on page 30.**

Applications

For Exercises 1–6, give the dimensions of each rectangle that can be made from the given number of tiles. Then use the dimensions of the rectangles to list all the factor pairs for each number.

1. 24   **2.** 32   **3.** 48   **4.** 45   **5.** 60   **6.** 72

7. What type of number has exactly two factors? Give examples.

8. What type of number has an odd number of factors? Give examples.

9. Luke has chosen a mystery number. His number is greater than 12 and less than 40, and it has exactly three factors. What might his number be? Use the display of rectangles for the numbers 1 to 30 from Problem 2.1 to help you find Luke's number. You may also need to think about what the displays for the numbers 31 to 40 would look like.

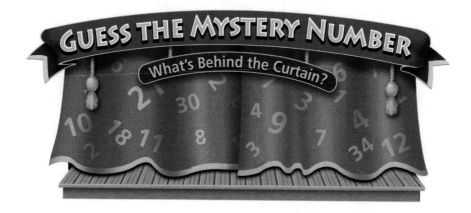

For Exercises 10–13, make a conjecture about whether each result will be odd or even. Use models, pictures, or other reasoning to support your conjectures.

10. An even number minus an even number

11. An odd number minus an odd number

12. An even number minus an odd number

13. An odd number minus an even number

14. How can you tell whether a number is even or odd? Explain or illustrate your answer in at least two ways.

15. How can you determine whether a sum of several numbers, such as $13 + 45 + 24 + 17$, is even or odd?

For: Help with Exercise 15
Web Code: ame-1215

16. Insert operation signs to make the answer correct.

   a. 2 ■ 5 ■ 3 = 17   **b.** 2 ■ 5 ■ 3 = 13

   c. 2 ■ 5 ■ 3 = 30   **d.** 2 ■ 5 ■ 3 = 7

17. Copy this Venn diagram and place whole numbers from 1 to 36 in the appropriate regions. Do you notice anything unusual about the diagram?

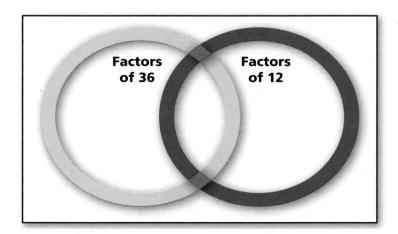

18. Copy this Venn diagram and find at least five numbers that belong in each region.

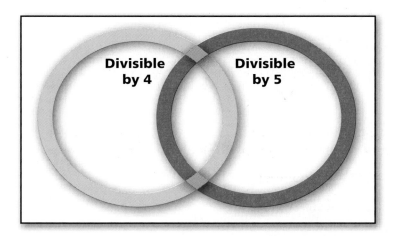

19. a. Draw and label a Venn diagram in which one circle represents the multiples of 3 and another circle represents the multiples of 5. Place whole numbers from 1 to 45 in the regions of the diagram.

  b. List four numbers between 1 and 45 that fall in the region outside the circles.

  c. The *common multiples* of 3 and 5 (the numbers that are multiples of both 3 and 5) should be in the intersection of the circles. What is the least common multiple of 3 and 5?

20. a. Draw and label a Venn diagram in which one circle contains the divisors of 42 and another circle contains the divisors of 60.

  b. The *common factors* of 42 and 60 (the numbers that are divisors of both 42 and 60) should be in the intersection of the circles. What is the greatest common factor of 42 and 60?

21. Find all the common multiples of 4 and 11 that are less than 100.

Connections

22. The Olympic photograph below inspired a school pep club to design card displays for football games. Each display uses 100 square cards, At a game, groups of 100 volunteers will hold up the cards to form complete pictures. They are most effective if the volunteers sit in a rectangular arrangements. What rectangular seating arrangements are possible? Which arrangements would you choose? Why?

23. A school band has 64 members. The band marches in the form of a rectangle. What rectangles can the band director make by arranging the members of the band? Which of these arrangements is most appealing to you? Why?

24. How many rectangles can you build with a prime number of square tiles?

25. **Multiple Choice** What is my number?

Clue 1 My number has two digits, and both digits are even.

Clue 2 The sum of my number's digits is 10.

Clue 3 My number has 4 as a factor.

Clue 4 The difference between the two digits of my number is 6.

A. 28   **B.** 46   **C.** 64   **D.** 72

26. a. List all the numbers less than or equal to 50 that are divisible by 5.

    b. Describe a pattern you see in your list that you can use to determine whether a large number—such as 1,276,549—is divisible by 5.

    c. Which numbers in your list are divisible by 2?

    d. Which numbers in your list are divisible by 10?

    e. How do the lists in parts (c) and (d) compare? Why does this result make sense?

27. Allie wants to earn some money for a new bike. She tells her dad she will wash the dishes for 2 cents on Monday, for 4 cents on Tuesday, and for 8 cents on Wednesday. If this pattern continued, how much would Allie earn on Thursday? How much would she earn altogether in 14 days?

28. Allie's eccentric aunt, May Belle, hides $10,000 in $20 bills under her mattress. If she spends one $20 bill every day, how many days will it take her to run out of bills?

29. a. What factor is paired with 6 to give 48?

    b. What factor is paired with 11 to give 121?

30. Using the terms *factor*, *divisor*, *multiple*, *product*, and *divisible by*, write as many statements as you can about the number sentence $6 \times 8 = 48$.

31. **Multiple Choice** Which number is a prime number?

    F. 91   **G.** 51   **H.** 31   **J.** 21

32. Multiple Choice Which number is a composite number?

    A. 2   **B.** 79   **C.** 107   **D.** 237

Go Online
PHSchool.com

For: Multiple-Choice Skills
Practice
Web Code: ama-1254

Extensions

33. Multiple Choice Which number is a square number?

    F. 128   **G.** 225   **H.** 360   **J.** 399

34. Find three numbers you can multiply to get 300.

35. a. Below is the complete list of the proper factors of a certain number. What is the number?

    1, 2, 3, 4, 6, 7, 12, 14, 21, 28, 42, 49, 84, 98, 147, 196, 294

    b. List each of the factor pairs for the number.

    c. How is the list of factor pairs related to the rectangles that could be made to show the number?

36. a. Find at least five numbers that belong in each region of the Venn diagram below.

    b. What do the numbers in the intersection have in common?

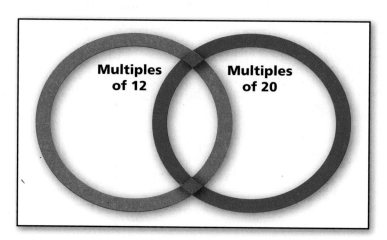

Consecutive numbers are whole numbers in a row, such as 31, 32, 33, or 52, 53, 54. Think of different series of consecutive numbers when you work on Exercises 37–40.

37. For any three consecutive numbers, what can you say about odd numbers and even numbers? Explain.

38. Mirari conjectures that, in every three consecutive whole numbers, one number would be divisible by 3. Do you think Mirari is correct? Explain.

39. How many consecutive numbers do you need to guarantee that one of the numbers is divisible by 5?

40. How many consecutive numbers do you need to guarantee that one of the numbers is divisible by 6?

41. Jeff is trying to determine when to quit looking for more whole number factors of a number. He has collected data about several numbers. For example, 30 has 1×30, 2×15, 3×10, 5×6, and then he can stop looking, because the factor pairs repeat. For 36, he can stop looking when he gets to 6×6. For 66, there are no new factor pairs after 6×11. Copy and complete the table below. Is there any pattern that would help him know when to stop looking?

Number	16	30	36	40	50	64	66
Last Factor Pair	■	5×6	6×6	■	■	■	6×11

Did You Know?

Many conjectures involving whole numbers seem simple, but are actually very difficult to justify. For example, in 1742, a mathematician named Christian Goldbach conjectured that any even number, except 2, could be written as the sum of two prime numbers. For example:

$$4 = 2 + 2 \qquad 12 = 7 + 5$$
$$36 = 17 + 19 \qquad 162 = 59 + 103$$

This seems like a pretty simple idea, doesn't it? However, in over 260 years, no one has been able to prove that it is true or find an even number that is not the sum of two prime numbers!

For: Information about Goldbach's Conjecture
PHSchool.com **Web Code:** ame-9031

Mathematical Reflections 2

In this investigation, you classified numbers, analyzed factor pairs, and made conjectures about sums and products of odd and even numbers. These questions will help you summarize what you have learned.

Think about your answers to these questions. Discuss your ideas with other students and your teacher. Then write a summary of your findings in your notebook.

1. Think about the grid paper models in Problem 2.1. For any number, how can you use grid paper models to find the factor pairs for that number?

2. What are Venn diagrams? How are they useful for showing relationships among numbers?

3. What strategy do you use to find a complete list of factors for a given number? How do you know when you have found all the possible factors?

4. What do you know about the sums and products of odd and even numbers? Justify your statements.

Unit Project What's Next?

Write about your special number. What can you say about your number now?

Is your number even? Is it odd?

How many factor pairs does your number have?

Investigation 3

Common Multiples and Common Factors

Many things happen over and over again in fixed cycles. For example, a morning news program may have a traffic report every 7 minutes. A train may arrive at a particular station every 12 minutes. A cuckoo clock may sound every 15 minutes.

How can you figure out when two events with different cycles can occur at the same time? Thinking about common factors and common multiples can help you solve such problems.

Let's start by comparing the multiples of 20 and 30.

- The multiples of 20 are 20, 40, 60, 80, 100, 120, 140, 160, 180, . . .
- The multiples of 30 are 30, 60, 90, 120, 150, 180, . . .

The numbers 60, 120, 180, 240, . . . , are multiples of both 20 and 30. We call these numbers **common multiples** of 20 and 30. Of these multiples, 60 is the *least common multiple*.

Now let's compare the factors of 12 and 30.

- The factors of 12 are 1, 2, 3, 4, 6, and 12.
- The factors of 30 are 1, 2, 3, 5, 6, 10, 15, and 30.

The numbers 1, 2, 3, and 6, are factors of both 12 and 30. We call these numbers **common factors** of 12 and 30. Of these factors, 6 is the *greatest common factor*.

3.1 Riding Ferris Wheels

One of the more popular rides at a carnival or amusement park is the Ferris wheel.

Problem 3.1 Choosing Common Multiples or Common Factors

Jeremy and his little sister, Deborah, are at a carnival. There are both a large and a small Ferris wheel. Jeremy gets on the large Ferris wheel at the same time his sister gets on the small Ferris wheel. The rides begin at the same time. For each situation below, decide how many seconds will pass before Jeremy and Deborah are both at the bottom again.

A. The large wheel makes one revolution in 60 seconds and the small wheel makes one revolution in 20 seconds.

B. The large wheel makes one revolution in 50 seconds and the small wheel makes one revolution in 30 seconds.

C. The large wheel makes one revolution in 10 seconds and the small wheel makes one revolution in 7 seconds.

D. For Questions A–C, determine the number of times each Ferris wheel goes around before Jeremy and his sister are both on the ground again.

ACE Homework starts on page 42.

3.2 Looking at Cicada Cycles

Cicadas (si KAY dahs) spend most of their lives underground. Some populations of cicadas come above ground every 13 years, while others come up every 17 years. Although cicadas do not cause damage directly to fruits and vegetables, they can damage orchards because the female makes slits in trees to lay her eggs.

Did You Know?

Cicadas are sometimes mistakenly called locusts. A locust is actually a type of grasshopper that looks nothing like a cicada. The error originated when early European settlers in North America encountered large outbreaks of cicadas. The swarms of insects reminded the settlers of stories they knew about swarms of locusts in Egypt.

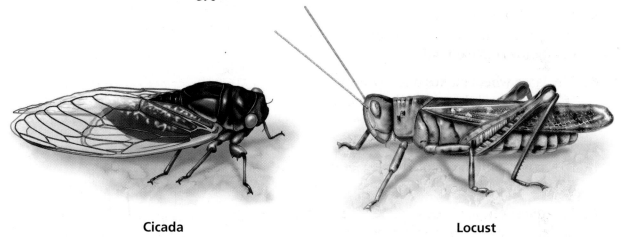

Cicada   **Locust**

Female cicadas lay their eggs in tree branches. When the young cicadas hatch, they drop to the ground and burrow into the soil. They remain underground for 13 or 17 years, feeding off juices from tree roots. Several months before they emerge, cicadas tunnel to the surface and wait to come out.

The mass emergence of cicadas is the key to their survival. There may be up to 1.5 million cicadas per acre! Many will be eaten by predators. However, enough will survive to lay eggs, so a new generation can emerge in 13 or 17 years.

Go Online
PHSchool.com **For:** Information about cicadas **Web Code:** ame-9031

Problem 3.2 Choosing Common Multiples or Common Factors

Stephan's grandfather told him about a terrible year when the cicadas were so numerous that they wrecked the buds on all the young trees in his orchard. Stephan conjectured that both 13-year and 17-year cicadas came up that year. Assume that Stephan's conjecture is correct.

A. How many years after an appearance of 13-year and 17-year cicadas together will both types of cicadas appear together again? Explain.

B. Suppose there were 12-year, 14-year, and 16-year cicadas, and they all came up this year. How many years will elapse before they all come up together again? Explain.

C. For Questions A and B, tell whether the answer is less than, greater than, or equal to the product of the cicada cycles.

ACE Homework starts on page 42.

3.3 Bagging Snacks

You have used common multiples to analyze events that repeat in cycles. Now you will explore problems about sharing items equally. Common factors can help you solve "sharing" problems.

Problem 3.3 Choosing Common Multiples or Common Factors

Jane and her friends are going on a hiking trip. Jane wants to make snack packs of apples and trail mix to take on the trip. She has 24 apples and 36 small bags of trail mix.

A. 1. What is the greatest number of snack packs Jane can make if each pack must have exactly the same number of apples and exactly the same number of bags of trail mix? She doesn't want any apples or trail mix left over. Explain.

2. Could Jane make a different number of snack packs so that the treats are shared equally? If so, describe each possibility.

3. Which possibility seems most reasonable to you? Why?

B. Suppose that Jane's pet canary has bitten into six of the packages of trail mix and ruined them. Now what is the greatest number of snack packs Jane can make so that the apples and the remaining trail mix are shared equally?

ACE Homework starts on page 42.

3.4 Planning a Picnic

Miriam's uncle runs a small convenience store. He often donates treats for Miriam's school parties.

Problem 3.4 Choosing Common Multiples or Common Factors

Miriam's uncle donated 120 cans of juice and 90 packs of cheese crackers for the school field trip. Each student is to receive the same number of cans of juice and the same number of packs of crackers.

A. What is the greatest number of students that can go on the field trip and share the food equally with no food left over? How many cans of juice and how many packs of crackers will each student receive? Explain.

B. Suppose Miriam's uncle eats two packs of crackers before he sends the supplies to school. What is the greatest number of students that can go on the field trip and share the food equally? How many cans of juice and how many packs of crackers will each student receive?

ACE Homework starts on page 42.

Applications

For Exercises 1–8, list the common multiples from 1 to 100 for each pair of numbers. Then find the least common multiple for each pair.

1. 8 and 12

2. 3 and 15

3. 7 and 11

4. 9 and 10

5. 24 and 36

6. 20 and 25

7. 42 and 14

8. 30 and 12

9. a. Find three pairs of numbers for which the least common multiple equals the product of the two numbers.

   b. Look at the pairs of numbers you found in part (a). What is true about all three pairs of numbers?

For Exercises 10–13, find two pairs of numbers with the given number as their least common multiple.

10. 10

11. 36

12. 60

13. 105

14. a. A restaurant is open 24 hours a day. The manager wants to divide the day into work shifts of equal length. The shifts should not overlap, and all shift durations should be a whole number of hours. Describe the different ways this can be done.

   b. The restaurant's two neon signs are turned on at the same time. Both signs blink as they are turned on. One sign blinks every 9 seconds. The other sign blinks every 15 seconds. In how many seconds will they blink together again?

15. The school cafeteria serves pizza every sixth day and applesauce every eighth day. If pizza and applesauce are both on today's menu, in how many days will they be together on the menu again?

For Exercises 16–23, list the common factors for each pair of numbers. Then find the greatest common factor for each pair.

For: Multiple-Choice Skills Practice
Web Code: ama-1354

16. 18 and 30

17. 9 and 25

18. 60 and 45

19. 23 and 29

20. 49 and 14

21. 140 and 25

22. 142 and 148

23. 84 and 105

24. **Multiple Choice** For which pair is the greatest common factor 8?

  A. 2 and 4

  B. 7 and 15

  C. 32 and 64

  D. 56 and 72

25. **Multiple Choice** For which pair is the greatest common factor 15?

  F. 60 and 75

  G. 30 and 60

  H. 10 and 25

  J. 3 and 5

26. **Multiple Choice** For which pair is the greatest common factor 1?

  A. 5 and 10

  B. 8 and 4

  C. 8 and 10

  D. 8 and 15

27. Mr. Mendoza and his 23 students are planning to have hot dogs at their class picnic. Mr. Mendoza can buy hot dogs in packages of 12 and hot dog buns in packages of 8.

For: Help with Exercise 27
Web Code: ame-1327

  a. Mr. Mendoza plans that everyone will get the same number of hot dogs and buns and there will be no leftovers. What are the least number of hot dog packages and the least number of bun packages Mr. Mendoza can buy? How many hot dogs and buns will each person get?

  b. Suppose that the class invites the principal, the secretary, the bus driver, and three parents to help supervise. How many packages of hot dogs and buns will Mr. Mendoza need to buy so that everyone will get the same number of hot dogs and buns with no leftovers? How many hot dogs and buns will each person get?

28. The cast of a play had a party at the drama teacher's house. There were 20 cookies and 40 carrot sticks served as refreshments. Each cast member had the same number of whole cookies and the same number of whole carrot sticks. Nothing was left over. The drama teacher did not eat. How many cast members might have been at the party? Explain.

29. Make up a word problem that you can solve by finding common factors. Then make up a different word problem that you can solve by finding common multiples. Solve your problems, and explain how you know that your answers are correct.

30. **Multiple Choice** Neena has 54 smiley-face stickers, 36 glittery stickers, and 81 heart stickers. She wants to divide the stickers evenly among her friends. Find the greatest number that Neena can use to divide the stickers evenly.

  F. 3   **G.** 9   **H.** 18   **J.** 27

Connections

31. Use the terms *factor, divisor, multiple, product,* and *divisible by* to write as many statements as you can about the number sentence below.

$$7 \times 9 = 63$$

32. **a.** What factor is paired with 12 to give 48?

  b. What factor is paired with 11 to give 110?

33. Use the fact that $135 \times 37 = 4{,}995$ to find the value of $1{,}350 \times 3{,}700$.

34. **a.** Suppose a jet travels 60 kilometers in 5 minutes. How many kilometers will it travel in 2 hours? In 6 hours?

  b. How many more kilometers will the jet travel in 6 hours than in 2 hours?

  c. Suppose that Nodin flew on this jet to the Dominican Republic. If his trip took 4 hours, how many kilometers did he travel?

35. Mario's watch runs fast. In 1 day, it gains an hour; so in 12 days, it gains 12 hours and is correct again. Julio's watch also runs fast. In 1 day, it gains 20 minutes. If they both set their 12-hour watches correctly at 9:00 A.M. on Monday, when will their watches both be correct again at the same time?

36. $3 \times 5 \times 7 = 105$. Use this fact to find each product.

    a. $9 \times 5 \times 7$ **b.** $3 \times 5 \times 14$

    c. $3 \times 50 \times 7$ **d.** $3 \times 25 \times 7$

Extensions

37. Ms. Santiago has many pens in her desk drawer. She says that if you divide the total number of pens by 2, 3, 4, 5, or 6, you get a remainder of 1. What is the smallest number of pens that could be in Ms. Santiago's drawer?

38. What is the mystery number pair?

    Clue 1   The greatest common factor of the mystery pair is 7.

    Clue 2   The least common multiple of the mystery pair is 70.

    Clue 3   Both of the numbers in the mystery pair have two digits.

    Clue 4   One of the numbers in the mystery pair is odd and the other is even.

39. Suppose that, in some distant part of the universe, there is a star with four orbiting planets. One planet makes a trip around the star in 6 Earth years, the second planet takes 9 Earth years, the third takes 15 Earth years, and the fourth takes 18 Earth years. Suppose that at some time the planets are lined up as pictured below. This phenomenon is called *conjunction*. How many years will it take before the planets return to this position?

40. Eric and his friends practice multiplying by using dominoes such as those above. Each half of a domino has dots on it to show a number from 0 to 6. The students use the two numbers on a domino as factors. So when Eric sees a domino like the one below, he answers 12.

  a. What is the greatest product you can make from numbers on dominoes?

  b. What is the least product you can make from numbers on dominoes?

  c. Eric reasons that he has to know the answers for $0 \times 0, 0 \times 1,$ $0 \times 2, 0 \times 3, 0 \times 4, 0 \times 5, 0 \times 6, 1 \times 0, 1 \times 1,$ and so on. Because there are seven different numbers, 0, 1, 2, 3, 4, 5, and 6, that can occur on each half of the domino, he reasons that he needs to know 49 different answers. This is too many. What did he forget?

41. Examine the number pattern below. You can use the tiles to help you see a pattern.

Row 1: 1	= 1	
Row 2: 1 + 3	= 4	
Row 3: 1 + 3 + 5	= 9	
Row 4: 1 + 3 + 5 + 7	= 16	

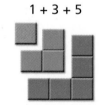

  a. Complete the next four rows in the number pattern.

  b. What is the sum in row 20?

  c. In what row will the sum be 576? What is the last number (addend) in the sum in this row? Explain.

Investigation 4

Factorizations: Searching for Factor Strings

Some numbers can be written as the product of several different pairs of factors. For example, 100 can be written as 1×100, 2×50, 4×25, 5×20, and 10×10. It is also possible to write 100 as the product of three factors, such as $2 \times 2 \times 25$ and $2 \times 5 \times 10$.

Getting Ready for Problem 4.1

Can you find a longer string of factors with a product of 100?

4.1 The Product Puzzle

The Product Puzzle is a number-search puzzle in which you look for strings of factors with a product of 840. Two factor strings have been marked in the puzzle at the right.

How many factor strings can you find?

The Product Puzzle

5	42	14	15	56	3
20	3	4	420	28	5
70	12	35	210	2	168
120	24	14	2	28	84
7	280	3	4	6	10
3	2	105	140	4	5
20	40	8	21	2	7

In the Product Puzzle, find as many factor strings for 840 as you can. When you find a string, draw a line through it. Keep a list of the strings you find.

A. What is the longest factor string you found?

B. If possible, name a factor string with a product of 840 that is longer than any string you found in the puzzle. Do not consider strings that contain 1.

C. Choose a factor string with two factors. How can you use this string to find a factor string with three factors?

D. How do you know when you have found the longest possible string of factors for a number?

E. How many distinct longest strings of factors are there for 840? Strings are *distinct* if they are different in some way other than the order in which the factors are listed.

ACE **Homework starts on page 56.**

The Product Puzzle

5	42	14	15	56	3
20	3	4	420	28	5
70	12	35	210	2	168
120	24	14	2	28	84
7	280	3	4	6	10
3	2	105	140	4	5
20	40	8	21	2	7

4.2 Finding the Longest Factor String

The strings of factors of a number are called **factorizations** of that number. In Problem 4.1, you saw that the longest possible factor string for 840 is made up of prime numbers. We call this string the **prime factorization** of 840. In fact, the longest factor string for any whole number is the prime factorization. Can you explain why?

Getting Ready for Problem 4.2

When you look for the prime factorization of a number, it helps to have a list of prime numbers handy. Look back at the table of first moves you made for the Factor Game. Make a list of all prime numbers less than 30.

One method for finding the prime factorization of a number is described below. In this example, you'll find the prime factorization of 100.

- First, find one prime factor of 100. You can start with 2. Divide 100 by 2, showing the work as an upside-down division problem.

$$2\,\big|\,\underline{100}$$
$$50$$

- Next, find a prime factor of 50. You can use 2 again. Add another step to the division problem.

$$2\,\big|\,\underline{100}$$
$$2\,\big|\,\underline{50}$$
$$25$$

- Now, find a prime factor of 25. The only possibility is 5.

$$2\,\big|\,\underline{100}$$
$$2\,\big|\,\underline{50}$$
$$5\,\big|\,\underline{25}$$
$$5$$

You are left with a prime number, 5. From the final diagram, you can read the prime factorization of 100: $100 = 2 \times 2 \times 5 \times 5$.

You could also use a *factor tree* to find the prime factorization of a number. Here are the steps to make a factor tree for 100.

- First, find a factor pair of 100. You might use 10 and 10. Write 100 and then draw branches from 100 to each factor.

$$100$$
$$10 \times 10$$

- If possible, break each factor you chose into the product of two factors. Draw branches to show how the factors are related to the numbers in the row above.

$$100$$
$$10 \times 10$$
$$5 \times 2 \times 5 \times 2$$

- Because all the numbers in the bottom row are prime, the tree is complete. The prime factorization of 100 is $5 \times 2 \times 5 \times 2$.

Here are two more factor trees for 100:

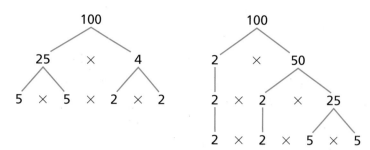

- In the tree at the right, notice that the 2 in the second row does not break down further. Draw a single branch, and repeat the 2 in the next rows.

You can see that the bottom row of each tree contains the same factors, although the order of the factors is different. You can also see that factor trees give you the same prime factorization for 100 as the previous method.

You can use a shorthand notation to write prime factorizations. For example, you can write $5 \times 5 \times 2 \times 2$ as $5^2 \times 2^2$. The small raised number is an exponent. An **exponent** tells you how many times a factor is used. For example, $2^2 \times 5^4$ means a 2 is used twice as a factor and a 5 is used four times. So, $2^2 \times 5^4$ is the same as $2 \times 2 \times 5 \times 5 \times 5 \times 5$.

You can read some exponents in more than one way.

Example	Ways to read
3^2	3 to the second power OR 3 squared
5^3	5 to the third power OR 5 cubed
2^4	2 to the fourth power

Problem 4.2 Finding the Longest Factor String

A. Why do we say *the* prime factorization of 100 instead of *a* prime factorization of 100?

B. Find the prime factorizations of 72, 120, and 600.

C. Write the prime factorizations of 72, 120, and 600 using exponents.

D. Choose a composite factor of 72.

   1. Show how this composite factor can be found in the prime factorization of 72.

   2. This composite factor is part of a factor pair for 72. How can you use the prime factorization to find the other factor in the pair?

E. Find a multiple of 72. What will the prime factorization of this multiple have in common with the prime factorization of 72?

ACE **Homework starts on page 56.**

Derrick wanted to find the common factors and common multiples of 24 and 60. He made Venn diagrams similar to the ones you made in Problem 2.3. He conjectured that he could use prime factorization to find common factors.

First, he found the prime factorizations of 24 and 60.

$$24 = 2 \times 2 \times 2 \times 3$$
$$60 = 2 \times 2 \times 3 \times 5$$

Both prime factorizations contain 2×2, which shows that 4 is a common factor.

$$24 = \boxed{2 \times 2} \times 2 \times 3$$
$$60 = \boxed{2 \times 2} \times 3 \times 5$$

Both prime factorizations contain 2×3, which shows that 6 is a common factor.

$$24 = 2 \times 2 \times \boxed{2 \times 3}$$
$$60 = 2 \times \boxed{2 \times 3} \times 5$$

Derrick noticed that the longest string common to both factorizations is $2 \times 2 \times 3$, so 12 must be the greatest common factor. He then checked a Venn Diagram and found that he was right.

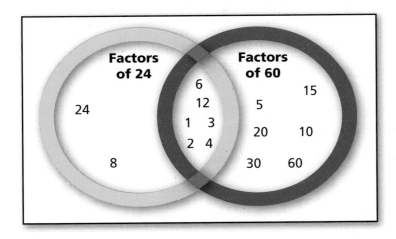

Derrick wondered if he could use a similar method to find the least common multiple. He realized that the prime factorization of any multiple of 24 will include its prime factorization, $2 \times 2 \times 2 \times 3$. The prime factorization of any multiple of 60 will contain its prime factorization, $2 \times 2 \times 3 \times 5$.

So, Derrick thought the prime factorization of any common multiple should include $2 \times 2 \times 2 \times 3 \times 5$. Is he right? Check this on the Venn diagram below:

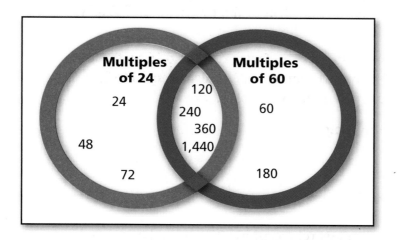

Problem 4.3 Using Prime Factorizations

A. 1. Write the prime factorizations of 72 and 120 that you found in Problem 4.2. What is the longest string common to both factorizations?

   2. What is the greatest common factor of 72 and 120? How do you know?

B. 1. What is the shortest string of factors that includes the prime factorizations of both 72 and 120? Can you find a smaller common multiple of 72 and 120? Why or why not?

   2. Can you find a greatest common multiple of 72 and 120? Why or why not?

C. Numbers whose greatest common factor is 1, such as 25 and 12, are **relatively prime.** How can you determine that 25 and 12 are relatively prime by looking at their prime factorizations? Find another pair of relatively prime numbers.

D. 1. Find two pairs of numbers whose least common multiple is the product of the numbers. For example, $5 \times 6 = 30$, and the least common multiple of 5 and 6 is 30.

   2. Find two pairs of numbers whose least common multiple is less than the product of the numbers. For example, $6 \times 8 = 48$, but the least common multiple of 6 and 8 is 24.

   3. How can you determine from the prime factorizations whether the least common multiple of two numbers is the product of the numbers or is less than the product of the two numbers? Explain your thinking.

E. If you multiply the greatest common factor of 12 and 16 by the least common multiple of 12 and 16, you get 192, which is equal to 12×16. Does this work for any two numbers? Why or why not?

ACE **Homework starts on page 56.**

Did You Know?

In all mathematics, there are a few relationships that are so basic that they are called *fundamental theorems*. There is the Fundamental Theorem of Calculus, the Fundamental Theorem of Algebra, and you have found the Fundamental Theorem of Arithmetic. The Fundamental Theorem of Arithmetic states that every whole number greater than one has exactly *one* prime factorization (except for the order in which the factors are written).

Go Online
PHSchool.com **For:** Information about fundamental theorems
Web Code: ame-9031

Applications

To solve a multiplication maze, you must find a path of numbers from the entrance to the exit so that the product of the numbers in the path equals the puzzle number. No diagonal moves are allowed. Below is the solution of a multiplication maze for 840.

Multiplication Maze 840

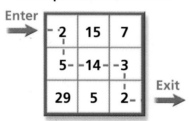

Solve each multiplication maze. **Hint: It may help to find the longest factor string of the puzzle number.**

1.   Multiplication Maze 840

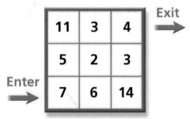

2.   Multiplication Maze 360

3. Make a multiplication maze for 720. Be sure to record your solution.

For Exercises 4–11, find the prime factorization of each number.

4. 36   **5.** 180   **6.** 525   **7.** 165

8. 293   **9.** 760   **10.** 216   **11.** 231

12. Use exponents to rewrite the prime factorizations you found in Exercises 4–11.

13. To indicate multiplication, you can use a raised dot symbol. For example, $3 \times 5 = 3 \cdot 5$. Find the prime factorization of 312 using raised dot symbols.

14. Multiple Choice What is the prime factorization of 240?

A. $10 \cdot 24$ **B.** $2 \cdot 3 \cdot 5$

C. $2^3 \cdot 3 \cdot 5$ **D.** $2^4 \cdot 3 \cdot 5$

15. Jill and Jamahl are comparing their special numbers. Jill's number has a prime factorization with six prime numbers. Jamahl's number has a prime factorization with only three numbers. Jill says this means her number is greater than Jamahl's. Jamahl says that is not necessarily true. Who is right?

16. Find all the numbers less than 100 that have at least one 2 and at least one 5 in their prime factorization. What do you notice about these numbers?

17. Multiple Choice Choose the number that is the product of exactly three different prime numbers.

F. 15   **G.** 20   **H.** 30   **J.** 57

Homework Help Online
PHSchool.com
For: Help with Exercise 18
Web Code: ame-1418

18. Find all the numbers less than 100 that are the product of exactly three different prime numbers.

For Exercises 19–24, find the greatest common factor and the least common multiple for each pair of numbers.

19. 36 and 45   **20.** 30 and 75   **21.** 78 and 104

22. 15 and 60   **23.** 32 and 45   **24.** 37 and 12

Connections

25. Mr. Rawlings has 60 cookies. He wants to give each of his 16 grandchildren the same number of cookies for a snack. What is the greatest number of cookies he can give each child? After he gives his grandchildren their cookies, how many cookies will he have left for himself?

26. Mr. and Mrs. Fisk have 8 children. Each of those children has 8 children. How many grandchildren do Mr. and Mrs. Fisk have? If each grandchild has 8 children, how many great-grandchildren do Mr. and Mrs. Fisk have?

27. Rosa claims the longest string of prime factors for 30 is 2 × 3 × 5. Tyee claims there is a longer string, 1 × 2 × 1 × 3 × 1 × 5. Who is correct? Why?

28. The number 1 is not prime. Why do you think mathematicians decided not to call 1 a prime number?

29. a. Find the multiples of 9 that are less than 100.

    b. Find the multiples of 21 that are less than 100.

    c. Find the common multiples of 9 and 21 that are less than 100.

    d. What is the next common multiple of 9 and 21?

Go Online
PHSchool.com
For: Multiple-Choice Skills Practice
Web Code: ama-1454

30. For each part below, use your birth year or the birth year of one of your family members as your number.

    a. Find the prime factorization of your number.

    b. Describe your number to a friend, giving your friend as much information as you can about the number. Here are some ideas to include: Is the number square, prime, even, or odd? How many factors does it have? Is it a multiple of some other number?

31. Tomas and Sharlina work on weekends and holidays doing odd jobs around the neighborhood. They are paid by the day, not the hour. They each earn the same whole number of dollars per day. Last month Tomas earned $184 and Sharlina earned $207. How many days did each person work? What is their daily pay?

32. What is my number?

    Clue 1 My number is a multiple of 2 and 7.

    Clue 2 My number is less than 100 but greater than 50.

    Clue 3 My number is the product of three different prime numbers.

33. What is my number?

    Clue 1 My number is a perfect square.

    Clue 2 The only prime number in its prime factorization is 2.

    Clue 3 My number is a factor of 32.

    Clue 4 The sum of its digits is odd.

Extensions

34. Most years contain 365 days, but certain years, called *leap years*, contain 366 days. Leap years occur in years divisible by four, with some exceptions. Years divisible by 100 are *not* leap years—unless they are divisible by 400. So 1896 was a leap year, but 1900 wasn't. Both 1996 and 2000 were leap years. A week has 7 days.

   a. How many weeks are in each type of year?

   b. January 1, 2004, fell on a Thursday. On what dates did the next three Thursdays of 2004 occur?

   c. The year 2004 was a leap year. It had 366 days. What day of the week was January 1, 2005?

   d. What is the pattern, over several years, for the days on which your birthday will fall?

35. The Fundamental Theorem of Arithmetic was first stated by the Greek mathematician Euclid. He wrote: "If a number is the least that is measured by prime numbers, it will not be measured by any prime except those originally measuring it." After studying prime factorizations in this Investigation, what do you suppose Euclid meant?

36. Mr. Barkley has a box of books. He says the number of books in the box is divisible by 2, 3, 4, 5, and 6. How many books could be in the box? Add another factor so that there is only one possible solution.

Did You Know?

If you were born on any day other than February 29, leap day, it takes at least 5 years for your birthday to come around to the same day of the week. It follows a pattern of 5 years, then 6 years, then 11 years, and then 6 years (or some variation of that pattern), to fall on the same day of the week. If you were born on February 29, it takes 28 years for your birthday to fall on the same day of the week!

Mathematical Reflections 4

In this investigation, you found factor strings for numbers, and you saw how the prime factorizations of numbers could be used to find common factors and multiples. These questions will help you summarize what you have learned.

Think about your answers to these questions. Discuss your ideas with other students and your teacher. Then write a summary of your findings in your notebook.

1. **a.** Does every number have a prime factorization?

   b. How many prime factorizations does a number have?

   c. Why is it important that 1 is not a prime number?

2. **a.** How can you use the prime factorization of two numbers to find their least common multiple? Give examples.

   b. How can you use the prime factorization of two numbers to find their greatest common factor? Give examples.

   c. How can you use the prime factorization of two numbers to determine whether they are relatively prime? Give examples.

3. If you know the greatest common factor of two numbers is 1, can you predict what the least common multiple will be?

Unit Project What's Next?

Don't forget your special number! What is its prime factorization?

Putting It All Together

Y ou have learned many things about factors and multiples of whole numbers. Now you'll have a chance to use what you know to solve an interesting problem.

5.1 Unraveling the Locker Problem

T here are 1,000 lockers in a long hall of Westfalls High. In preparation for the beginning of school, the janitor cleans the lockers and paints fresh numbers on the locker doors. The lockers are numbered from 1 to 1,000. When the 1,000 Westfalls High students return from summer vacation, they decide to celebrate the beginning of the school year by working off some energy.

The first student, Student 1, runs down the row of lockers and opens every door.

Student 2 closes the doors of Lockers 2, 4, 6, 8, and so on to the end of the line.

Student 3 *changes the state of* the doors of Lockers 3, 6, 9, 12, and so on to the end of the line. (This means the student opens the door if it is closed and closes the door if it is open.)

Student 4 changes the state of the doors of Lockers 4, 8, 12, 16, and so on.

active math
online

For: Locker Problem Activity
Visit: PHSchool.com
Web Code: amd-1501

Student 5 changes the state of every fifth door, Student 6 changes the state of every sixth door, and so on, until all 1,000 students have had a turn.

Getting Ready for Problem

Consider this question:

When all the students have finished, which locker doors are open?

Make a conjecture about the answer to this question. Then, describe a strategy you might use to try to find the answer.

A famous mathematician, George Polya, wrote a book titled *How to Solve It* about problem-solving strategies. He suggests that if you can't solve a problem right away, you might first try to solve a related problem or a simplified version of the problem so that you can look for patterns and strategies to help you. He also suggests drawing pictures. Professor Polya solved some very complicated math problems that way!

Go **Online**
PHSchool.com
For: Information about prime numbers
Web Code: ame-9031

Problem 5.1 Using Multiples and Factors

A. Model the problem for the first 30 students and the first 30 lockers. What patterns do you see as the students put their plan into action?

B. When the 1,000 students are finished, which locker doors are open? Explain why your answer makes sense. What kind of numbers are these?

C. Give the numbers of several lockers that were touched by exactly

  1. two students. What kind of numbers are these?

  2. three students.

  3. four students.

D. How can you determine exactly how many students have touched a given locker?

E. Which was the first locker touched by

  1. both Student 6 and Student 8?

  2. both Student 12 and Student 30?

  3. both Student 7 and Student 13?

  4. both Student 100 and Student 120?

F. Given two student numbers, how can you determine which locker will be the first touched by both students? How can you determine which locker will be the last touched by both students?

G. Which students touched

  1. both Locker 24 and Locker 36?

  2. both Locker 100 and Locker 120?

  3. both Locker 42 and Locker 273?

H. Given two lockers, how can you determine which students touched both?

ACE Homework starts on page 65.

Applications

Applications

Connections

Extensions

Applications

For Exercises 1–3, refer to Problem 5.1.

1. Give the numbers of several lockers that were touched by exactly five students.

2. Which was the first locker touched by both

   a. Students 3 and 5?

   b. Students 12 and 20?

   c. Students 72 and 84?

   d. Students 210 and 315?

3. Which students touched both

   a. Lockers 13 and 81?

   b. Lockers 140 and 210?

   c. Lockers 165 and 330?

   d. Lockers 196 and 294?

Connections

4. There are 50 lockers, numbered 1 through 50, in a short hall at Phillips Middle School. Mr. Giannetti hid treats for his class in one of the lockers. He gave the class the following clues about the number of the locker where the treats are located.

   Clue 1 The number is even.

   Clue 2 The number is divisible by 3.

   Clue 3 The number is a multiple of Mr. Giannetti's lucky number, 7.

   In which locker are the treats located?

5. How many factors does each of the following numbers have?

    a. 100   **b.** 101   **c.** 102   **d.** 103

6. Write a mathematical story about the number 648. For example, you might describe its factors and its multiples. You might also give some examples of its relationship to other numbers. Use at least five vocabulary words from this unit in your story.

7. What is the least prime number greater than 50?

8. Ivan said that if a number ends in 0, both 2 and 5 are factors of the number. Is he correct? Why or why not?

For: Help with Exercise 8
Web Code: ame-1508

9. What is my number?

    Clue 1 My number is a multiple of 5 and is less than 50.

    Clue 2 My number is a multiple of 3.

    Clue 3 My number has exactly 8 factors.

10. What is my number?

    Clue 1 My number is a multiple of 5, but it does not end in 5.

    Clue 2 The prime factorization of my number is a string of three numbers.

    Clue 3 Two of the numbers in the prime factorization are the same.

    Clue 4 My number is greater than the seventh square number.

11. Now it's your turn! Make up a set of clues for a mystery number. You might want to use your special number as the mystery number. Include as many ideas from this unit as you can. Try out your clues on a classmate.

For Exercises 12 and 13, describe the numbers that have both of the given numbers as factors.

12. 2 and 3   **13.** 3 and 5

Go Online
PHSchool.com
For: Multiple-Choice Skills Practice
Web Code: ama-1554

14. a. Find all the numbers between 1 and 1,000 that have 2 as their only prime factor.

    b. What is the next number after 1,000 that has 2 as its only prime factor?

15. The numbers 2 and 3 are prime, consecutive numbers. Are there other such pairs of *adjacent primes*? Why or why not?

16. Which group of numbers—evens or odds—contains more prime numbers? Why?

Extensions

17. Goldbach's Conjecture is a famous conjecture that has never been proved true or false. The conjecture states that every even number, except 2, can be written as the sum of two prime numbers. For example, 16 can be written as 5 + 11, which are both prime numbers.
  a. Write the first six even numbers greater than 2 as the sum of two prime numbers.
  b. Write 100 as the sum of two primes.
  c. The number 2 is a prime number. Can an even number greater than 4 be written as the sum of two prime numbers if you use 2 as one of the primes? Why or why not?

18. Multiple Choice Choose the number that is divisible by four different prime numbers.
  A. 77   **B.** 105   **C.** 225   **D.** 1,155

19. Find the least number that is divisible by four different prime numbers.

20. Prime numbers that differ by 2, such as 3 and 5, are called *twin primes*. Starting with the twin primes 5 and 7, look carefully at the numbers between twin primes. What do they have in common? Why?

21. Try to discover a method for finding all the factors of a number using its prime factorization. Use your method to find all the factors of 36. Then use your method to find all the factors of 480.

22. Suppose a number has 2 and 6 as factors. What other numbers must be factors of the number? Explain.

23. Suppose a number is a multiple of 12. Of what other numbers is it a multiple? Explain.

24. Suppose 10 and 6 are common factors of two numbers. What other factors must the numbers have in common? Explain.

25. The chart below shows the factor counts for the numbers from 975 to 1,000. Each star stands for one factor. For example, the four stars after 989 indicate that 989 has four factors.

975	★★★★★★★★★★★★
976	★★★★★★★★★★
977	★★
978	★★★★★★★★
979	★★★★
980	★★★★★★★★★★★★★★★★★★
981	★★★★★★
982	★★★★
983	★★
984	★★★★★★★★★★★★★★★★
985	★★★★
986	★★★★★★★★
987	★★★★★★★★
988	★★★★★★★★★★★★
989	★★★★
990	★★★★★★★★★★★★★★★★★★★★★★★★
991	★★
992	★★★★★★★★★★★★
993	★★★★
994	★★★★★★★★
995	★★★★
996	★★★★★★★★★★★★
997	★★
998	★★★★
999	★★★★★★★★
1,000	★★★★★★★★★★★★★★★★

Boris thinks that numbers that have many factors, such as 975 and 996, must be abundant numbers. (Recall that an *abundant number* is a number whose proper factors have a sum greater than the number.) Is Boris correct? Explain.

Mathematical Reflections 5

Working on the locker problem gave you an opportunity to use what you know about whole numbers, factors, and multiples. These questions will help you summarize what you have learned.

Think about your answers to these questions. Discuss your ideas with other students and your teacher. Then write a summary of your findings in your notebook.

1. What can you say about a number if all you know is that it has an odd number of factors? Justify your answer.

2. Describe how the following ideas were used in solving parts of the Locker Problem:
   a. prime numbers
   b. divisors
   c. multiples
   d. square numbers
   e. least common multiple
   f. greatest common factor

Unit Project   What's Next?

Don't forget your special number. What new things can you say about your number?

Unit Project

My Special Number

At the beginning of this unit, you chose a special number and wrote several things about it in your journal. As you worked through the investigations, you used the concepts you learned to write new things about your number.

Now it is time for you to show off your special number. Write a story, compose a poem, make a poster, or find some other way to highlight your number.

Your teacher will use your project to determine how well you understand the concepts in this unit, so be sure to include all the things you have learned while working through the investigations. You may want to start by looking back through your journal to find the things you wrote after each investigation. In your project, be sure you use all the vocabulary your teacher has asked you to record in your journals for *Prime Time*.

Looking Back and Looking Ahead

While working on the problems in this unit, you investigated some important properties of whole numbers. Finding factors and multiples of numbers and identifying prime numbers helps in answering questions about clocks and calendars, puzzles and games, and rectangular patterns of tiles. Factoring also focuses attention on the properties of even and odd numbers, square numbers, greatest common factors, and least common multiples.

Go Online
PHSchool.com
For: Vocabulary Review Puzzle
Web Code: amj-1051

Use Your Understanding: Number Patterns

Test your understanding of multiples, factors, and prime numbers, by solving the following problems.

1. The Red Top Taxi company wants to keep its cars in good operating condition. It has a schedule for regular maintenance checks on each car. Oil is to be changed once every 6 weeks. Brakes are to be inspected and repaired every 10 weeks.

   a. After a new cab is put in service, is there ever a week when that cab is scheduled for both an oil change and a brake inspection? If so, what is the first such time?

   b. Suppose the oil change time is extended to 8 weeks and the brake inspection to 12 weeks. Is there ever a week when the cab is due for both an oil change and brake inspection? If so, when will such a coincidence first occur?

2. The Mystate University marching band consists of 60 members. The band director wants to arrange the band into a rectangular array for the halftime activities.

   a. In how many ways can she arrange the band? Make a sketch of each arrangement.

   b. How many rectangular arrangements are possible if the band adds one member and becomes a 61-member band?

3. The prime factorization of Tamika's special number is $2 \times 2 \times 3 \times 11$ and the prime factorization of Cyrah's special number is $3 \times 3 \times 5 \times 5$.

   a. What is the least common multiple of the two special numbers?

   b. What is the greatest common factor of the two special numbers?

   c. List all the factors of Tamika's number.

   d. Is Tamika's number even or odd? Is Cyrah's number even or odd?

   e. Is Tamika's number a square number? Is Cyrah's number a square number?

4. Shani gave three clues for her secret number.

   Clue 1 *My number is a factor of 90.*

   Can you determine what Shani's secret number is?

   a. What is the smallest Shani's number can be? What is the largest Shani's number can be?

   b. Brandon says the secret number must also be a factor of 180. Is he correct?

   Clue 2 *My number is prime.*

   c. Now can you determine what the secret number is?

   Clue 3 *Twenty-one is a multiple of my secret number.*

   d. Now can you determine what the secret number is?

Explain Your Reasoning

To answer Questions 1–4 you had to use knowledge of factors and multiples of a number.

5. What strategies can be used to find

   a. all the factors of a number?

   b. the least common multiple of two numbers?

   c. the greatest common factor of two numbers?

6. How you can you decide whether a number is a(n)

   a. prime number?

   b. square number?

   c. even number?

   d. odd number?

7. Decide whether each statement is *true* or *false*. Explain your reasoning. (A statement is true if it is correct for *every* pair of numbers. If you can find a pair of numbers that makes the statement incorrect, then the statement is false.)

   a. If a number is greater than a second number, then the first number has more factors than the second number.

   b. The sum of two odd numbers is even.

   c. The product of an even number and an odd number is odd.

   d. The least common multiple of two different prime numbers is the product of those numbers.

   e. The greatest common factor of two numbers is less than either of those numbers.

Look Ahead

You will use ideas about factors, multiples, and primes in many future units of *Connected Mathematics*, especially those that deal with properties of other numbers like fractions and decimals.

English/Spanish Glossary

A

abundant number A number for which the sum of all its proper factors is greater than the number itself. For example, 24 is an abundant number because its proper factors, 1, 2, 3, 4, 6, 8, and 12, add to 36.

número abundante Un número con factores propios que sumados resultan en un número mayor que el número mismo. Por ejemplo, 24 es un número abundante porque la suma de sus factores propios, 1, 2, 3, 4, 6, 8 y 12, es 36.

C

common factor A factor that two or more numbers share. For example, 7 is a common factor of 14 and 35 because 7 is a factor of 14 ($14 = 7 \times 2$) and 7 is a factor of 35 ($35 = 7 \times 5$).

factor común Un factor que es compartido por dos o más números. Por ejemplo, 7 es factor común de 14 y 35 porque 7 es factor de 14 ($14 = 7 \times 2$) y 7 es factor de 35 ($35 = 7 \times 5$).

common multiple A multiple that two or more numbers share. For example, the first few multiples of 5 are 5, 10, 15, 20, 25, 30, 35, 40, 45, 50, 55, 60, 65, and 70. The first few multiples of 7 are 7, 14, 21, 28, 35, 42, 49, 56, 63, 70, 77, 84, 91, and 98. From these lists, we can see that two common multiples of 5 and 7 are 35 and 70.

múltiplo común Un múltiplo compartido por dos o más números. Por ejemplo, los primeros múltiplos de 5 son 5, 10, 15, 20, 25, 30, 35, 40, 45, 50, 55, 60, 65 y 70. Los primeros múltiplos de 7 son 7, 14, 21, 28, 35, 42, 49, 56, 63, 70, 77, 84, 91 y 98. Estas listas nos indican que dos múltiplos comunes de 5 y 7 son el 35 y el 70.

composite number A whole number with factors other than itself and 1 (that is, a whole number that is not prime). Some composite numbers are 6, 12, 20, and 1,001.

número compuesto Un número entero con otros factores además del número mismo y el 1 (es decir, un número entero que no es primo). Algunos números compuestos son 6, 12, 20 y 1,001.

conjecture A guess about a pattern or relationship based on observations.

conjetura Suposición acerca de un patrón o relación, basada en observaciones.

deficient number A number for which the sum of all its proper factors is less than the number itself. For example, 14 is a deficient number because its proper factors, 1, 2, and 7, add to 10. All prime numbers are deficient.

número deficiente Un número con factores propios que sumados resultan en un número menor que el número mismo. Por ejemplo, 14 es un número deficiente porque la suma de sus factores 1, 2 y 7 equivale a 10. Todos los números primos son deficientes.

dimensions The dimensions of a rectangle are the lengths of its sides. For example, the rectangle below has side lengths of 5 and 3. We can refer to this rectangle as a 5 × 3 rectangle.

dimensiones Las dimensiones de un rectángulo son las longitudes de sus lados. Por ejemplo, el rectángulo de abajo tiene longitudes de lados de 3 y 5. Podemos referirnos a este rectángulo como un rectángulo de 5 × 3.

divisor A number that divides a given number leaving a zero remainder. For example, 5 is a divisor of 20 since 20 ÷ 5 = 4 has a remainder of 0. A divisor of a given number is also known as a factor of that number. Another way to determine if 5 is a divisor of 20 is to ask whether there is a whole number that, when multiplied by 5, gives 20. The number is 4. 5 × 4 = 20.

divisor Número que divide a otro número sin dejar ningún resto. Por ejemplo, 5 es un divisor de 20 porque 20 ÷ 5 = 4 tiene resto cero. El divisor de un número determinado también se conoce como un factor de ese número. Otra manera de determinar si 5 es divisor de 20 es preguntando si hay un número entero que, al ser multiplicado por 5, dé 20. El número es 4. 5 × 4 = 20.

even number A multiple of 2. When you divide an even number by 2, the remainder is 0. Examples of even numbers are 0, 2, 4, 6, 8, and 10.

número par Un múltiplo de 2. Cuando divides un número par por 2, el resto es 0. Los siguientes son ejemplos de números pares: 0, 2, 4, 6, 8 y 10.

exponent The small raised number that tells how many times a factor is used. For example, 5^3 means 5 × 5 × 5. 3 is the exponent.

exponente El pequeño número elevado que dice cuántas veces se usa un factor. Por ejemplo, 5^3 significa 5 × 5 × 5. 3 es el exponente.

factor One of two or more whole numbers that are multiplied to get a product. For example, 13 and 4 are both factors of 52 because $13 \times 4 = 52$.

factor Uno de dos o más números enteros que se multiplican para obtener un producto. Por ejemplo, tanto 13 como 4 son factores de 52 porque $13 \times 4 = 52$.

factor pair Two whole numbers that are multiplied to get a product. For example, in the pair 13, 4 is a factor pair of 52 because $13 \times 4 = 52$.

par de factores Dos números enteros que se multiplican para obtener un producto. Por ejemplo, el par 13, 4 es un par factor de 52 porque $13 \times 4 = 52$.

factorization A product of numbers, perhaps with some repetitions, resulting in the desired number. A number can have many factorizations. For example, two factorizations of 60 are 3×20 and $2 \times 2 \times 15$.

factorización Producto de números, con posibles repeticiones, que resultan en el número deseado. Un número puede tener muchas factorizaciones. Por ejemplo, dos factorizaciones de 60 son 3×20 y $2 \times 2 \times 15$.

Fundamental Theorem of Arithmetic The theorem stating that, except for the order of the factors, every whole number greater than 1 can be factored into prime factors in only one way.

Teorema fundamental de la aritmética Teorema que enuncia que, salvo por el orden de los factores, todos los números enteros mayores de 1 pueden descomponerse en factores primos de una sola manera.

greatest common factor The greatest factor that two or more numbers share. For example, 1, 2, 3, and 6 are common factors of 12 and 30, but 6 is the greatest common factor.

máximo común factor El factor mayor que comparten dos o más números. Por ejemplo, 1, 2, 3 y 6 son factores comunes de 12 y 30, pero 6 es el máximo común factor.

least common multiple The least multiple that two or more numbers share. Common multiples of 6 and 8 include 24, 48, and 72, but 24 is the least common multiple.

mínimo común múltiplo El múltiplo menor que comparten dos o más números. Los múltiplos comunes de 6 y 8 incluyen 24, 48 y 72, pero 24 es el mínimo común múltiplo.

multiple The product of a given whole number and another whole number. For example, some multiples of 3 are 3, 6, 9, and 12. Note that if a number is a multiple of 3, then 3 is a factor of the number. For example, 12 is a multiple of 3, and 3 is a factor of 12.

múltiplo El producto de un número entero dado y otro número entero. Por ejemplo, algunos múltiplos de 3 son 3, 6, 9 y 12. Observa que si un número es múltiplo de 3, entonces 3 es factor de ese número. Por ejemplo, 12 es múltiplo de 3, y 3 es factor de 12.

near-perfect number A number for which the sum of all its proper factors is one less than the number. All powers of 2 are near-perfect numbers. For example, 32 is a near-perfect number because its proper factors, 1, 2, 4, 8, and 16, add to 31.

número casi perfecto Un número con factores propios que sumados resultan en 1 menos que ese número. Todas las potencias de 2 son números casi perfectos. Por ejemplo, 32 es un número casi perfecto porque sus factores propios 1, 2, 4, 8 y 16 suman 31.

odd number A whole number that is not a multiple of 2. When an odd number is divided by 2, the remainder is 1. Examples of odd numbers are 1, 3, 5, 7, and 9.

número impar Un número entero que no es múltiplo de 2. Cuando un número impar se divide por 2, el resto es 1. Los siguientes son ejemplos de números impares: 1, 3, 5, 7 y 9.

perfect number A number for which the sum of all its proper factors is the number itself. For example, 6 is a perfect number because its proper factors, 1, 2, and 3, add to 6.

número perfecto Un número con factores propios que, cuando se suman, el resultado es ese número exacto. Por ejemplo, 6 es un número perfecto porque la suma de sus factores propios, 1, 2 y 3, es 6.

prime factorization A product of prime numbers, perhaps with some repetitions, resulting in the desired number. For example, the prime factorization of 7,007 is $7 \times 7 \times 11 \times 13$. The prime factorization of a number is unique except for the order of the factors.

descomposición en factores primos Un producto de números primos, con posibles repeticiones, que resulta en el número deseado. Por ejemplo, la descomposición en factores primos de 7,007 es $7 \times 7 \times 11 \times 13$. La descomposición en factores primos de un número es única salvo por el orden de los factores.

prime number A number with exactly two factors, 1 and the number itself. Examples of primes are 11, 17, 53, and 101. The number 1 is not a prime number because it has only one factor.

número primo Un número que tiene exactamente dos factores: 1 y él mismo. Los siguientes son ejemplos de números primos: 11, 17, 53 y 101. El número 1 no es un número primo porque tiene sólo un factor.

proper factors All the factors of a number, except the number itself. For example, the proper factors of 16 are 1, 2, 4, and 8.

factores propios Todos los factores de un número salvo el número mismo. Por ejemplo, los factores propios de 16 son 1, 2, 4 y 8.

relatively prime numbers A pair of numbers with no common factors except for 1. For example, 20 and 33 are relatively prime because the factors of 20 are 1, 2, 4, 5, 10, and 20, while the factors of 33 are 1, 3, 11, and 33. Notice that neither 20 nor 33 is itself a prime number.

números relativamente primos Par de números que no tienen factores comunes salvo 1. Por ejemplo, 20 y 33 son números relativamente primos porque los factores de 20 son 1, 2, 4, 5, 10 y 20 mientras que los factores de 33 son 1, 3, 11 y 33. Observa que ni el 20 ni el 33 son en sí mismos números primos.

square number A number that is a result of the product of a number multiplied by itself. For example, 9 and 64 are square numbers because $9 = 3 \times 3$ and $64 = 8 \times 8$. A square number represents a number of square tiles that can be arranged to form a square.

número al cuadrado Número que es el resultado del producto de un número multiplicado por sí mismo. Por ejemplo, 9 y 64 son números al cuadrado porque $9 = 3 \times 3$ y $64 = 8 \times 8$. Un número al cuadrado representa un número de mosaicos cuadrados que se pueden colocar para formar un cuadrado.

Venn diagram A diagram in which overlapping circles are used to show relationships among sets of objects that have certain attributes. Two examples are shown below.

diagrama de Venn Un diagrama en el que se usan círculos superpuestos para representar relaciones entre conjuntos de objetos que tienen ciertos atributos. A continuación se muestran dos ejemplos. En uno se muestran factores de 24 y factores de 60, y en el otro se muestran múltiplos de 24 y múltiplos de 60.

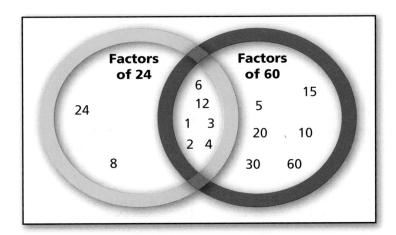

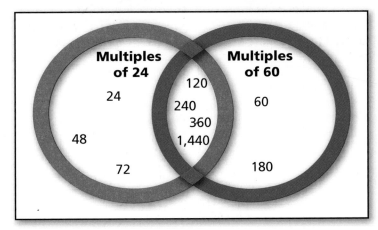

English/Spanish Glossary

Academic Vocabulary

Academic vocabulary words are words that you see in textbooks and on tests. These are not math vocabulary terms, but knowing them will help you succeed in mathematics.

Las palabras de vocabulario académico son palabras que ves en los libros de texto y en las pruebas. Éstos no son términos de vocabulario de matemáticas, pero conocerlos te ayudará a tener éxito en matemáticas.

D

determine To use the given information and any related facts to find a value or make a decision.
related terms: decide, find, calculate, conclude

Sample: What is one way to determine the prime factorization of 27?

I could use a factor tree to determine the prime factorization of 27.

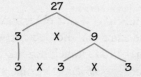

I can also divide 27 by prime numbers until I have a prime quotient. For example, 3 is prime and 27 ÷ 3 = 9. Since 9 is not prime, I continue to divide. 9 ÷ 3 = 3 and 3 is prime. The prime factors for 27 are 3 × 3 × 3.

determinar Usar la información dada y cualesquiera datos relacionados para hallar un valor o tomar una decisión.
términos relacionados: decidir, hallar, calcular, concluir

Ejemplo: ¿Cuál es una forma de determinar la descomposición en factores primos de 27?

Podría usar un árbol de factores para determinar la descomposición en factores primos de 27.

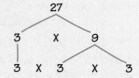

También puedo dividir 27 por números primos hasta obtener el cociente primo. Por ejemplo, 3 es un número primo y 27 ÷ 3 = 9. Puesto que 9 no es un número primo, puedo continuar con la división. 9 ÷ 3 = 3 y 3 es un número primo. Los factores primos de 27 son 3 × 3 × 3.

E

explain To give facts and details that make an idea easier to understand. Explaining can involve a written summary supported by a diagram, chart, table, or a combination of these.
related terms: analyze, clarify, describe, justify, tell

Sample: Amara is thinking of a number that is the least common multiple of 5 and 6. What is the number? Explain your reasoning.

Multiples of 5: 5, 10, 15, 20, 25, 30, 35...
Multiples of 6: 6, 12, 18, 24, 30, 36, 42...
The first common multiple is 30. So, Amara's number is 30.

explicar Dar hechos y detalles que hacen que una idea sea más fácil de comprender. Explicar puede implicar un resumen escrito apoyado por hechos, un diagrama, una gráfica, una tabla o una combinación de éstos.
términos relacionados: analizar, aclarar, describir, justificar, decir

Ejemplo: Amara está pensando en un número que es el mínimo común múltiplo de 5 y 6. ¿Cuál es el número? Explica tu razonamiento.

Múltiplos de 5: 5, 10, 15, 20, 25, 30, 35...
Múltiplos de 6: 6, 12, 18, 24, 30, 36, 42...
El primer común múltiplo es 30. Así que el número de Amara es 30.

J

justify To support your answers with reasons or examples
related terms: validate, explain, defend

Sample: Jeffrey claims that 12 and 14 are relatively prime numbers. Is Jeffrey correct? Justify your answer.

Jeffrey is not correct. The Venn diagram shows that 12 and 14 have both 1 and 2 as common factors. Since 12 and 14 share two factors they cannot be relatively prime.

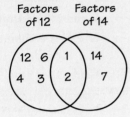

Factors   Factors
of 12   of 14

justificar Apoyar tus respuestas con razones o ejemplos.
términos relacionados: validar, explicar, defender

Ejemplo: Jeffrey afirma que 12 y 14 son números primos entre sí. ¿Es correcta la afirmación de Jeffrey? Justifica tu respuesta.

La afirmación de Jeffrey no es correcta. El diagrama de Venn muestra que 12 y 14 tienen 1 y 2 como factores comunes. Puesto que 12 y 14 comparten dos factores no pueden ser números primos entre sí.

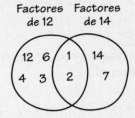

Factores   Factores
de 12   de 14

R

represent To stand for or take the place of something else. Symbols, equations, charts, and tables are often used to represent particular situations.
related terms: symbolize, stand for

Sample: Which of the following sets of numbers represents the factors of 16? Explain.

A. {1, 2, 3, 4, 9, 16}   C. {1, 2, 4, 8, 16}

B. {2, 4, 8}   D. {16, 32, 48, 64}

Set C represents the factors of 16. Set A does not represent the factors of 16 since 3 and 9 are not factors of 16. Set B does not include 1 and 16, which are factors of 16. Set D contains multiples of 16 instead of factors of 16.

representar Significar o tomar el lugar de algo más. Con frecuencia se usan símbolos, ecuaciones, gráficas y tablas para representar situaciones particulares.
términos relacionados: simbolizar, significar

Ejemplo: ¿Cuál de los siguientes conjuntos de números representa los factores de 16? Explica tu respuesta.

A. {1, 2, 3, 4, 9, 16}   C. {1, 2, 4, 8, 16}

B. {2, 4, 8}   D. {16, 32, 48, 64}

El conjunto C representa los factores de 16. El conjunto A no representa los factores de 16 puesto que 3 y 9 no son factores de 16. El conjunto B no incluye 1 y 16, los cuales son factores de 16. El conjunto D contiene múltiplos de 16 en lugar de factores de 16.

Academic Vocabulary

Index

Index

Acknowledgments

Team Credits

The people who made up the **Connected Mathematics2** team—representing editorial, editorial services, design services, and production services—are listed below. Bold type denotes core team members.

Leora Adler, Judith Buice, Kerry Cashman, Patrick Culleton, Sheila DeFazio, Richard Heater, **Barbara Hollingdale, Jayne Holman,** Karen Holtzman, **Etta Jacobs,** Christine Lee, Carolyn Lock, Catherine Maglio, **Dotti Marshall,** Rich McMahon, Eve Melnechuk, Kristin Mingrone, Terri Mitchell, **Marsha Novak,** Irene Rubin, Donna Russo, Robin Samper, Siri Schwartzman, **Nancy Smith,** Emily Soltanoff, **Mark Tricca,** Paula Vergith, Roberta Warshaw, Helen Young

Additional Credits

Diana Bonfilio, Mairead Reddin, Michael Torocsik, nSight, Inc.

Technical Illustration

WestWords, Inc.

Cover Design

tom white.images

Photos

2, Frank Cezus/Getty Images, Inc.; **3 t,** Adrian Peacock/ImageState; **3 b,** Peter Hvizdak/The Image Works; **5,** Richard Haynes; **6 t,** Michael Newman/PhotoEdit; **6 bl,** BananaStock/SuperStock; **6 bm,** Michael Newman/PhotoEdit; **6 br,** Ryan McVay/Getty Images, Inc.; **10,** Declan McCullagh Photography; **13,** Richard Haynes; **17,** Frank Cezus/Getty Images, Inc.; **22,** Rex Butcher/Getty Images, Inc.; **25,** Richard Haynes; **32,** Bettmann/Corbis; **37,** Lester Lefkowitz/Corbis; **38,** Ron Chapple/Thinkstock/Alamy Images; **41,** Ariel Skelley/Corbis; **42,** joSon/SuperStock; **47,** ©1991 by Sydney Harris, From "You Want Proof, I'll Give You Proof!", WH. Freeman, New York; **57,** Peter Usbeck/Alamy Images; **58,** David Young-Wolff/PhotoEdit; **65,** Digital Vision/Getty Images, Inc.; **66,** Richard Haynes

Data Sources

Information on Prime Numbers on pages 10-11 from THE NEW YORK TIMES, August 8, 2002. Copyright © 2002 The New York Times Company.